COME
HELL

OR HIGH
WATER

by Melvina W.

Copyright © 2024 Melvina Washington

Self Publishing Services provided by Krystal Lee Enterprises LLC (KLE Publishing)

All rights reserved. No parts of this book may be reproduced, distributed, or used in any manner, including photocopying, recording, or other electronic or mechanical methods without the prior written permission of the copywriter owner, except for the use of brief quotations in a book review and certain noncommercial uses permitted by copyright law.

Paperback: 978-1-945066-50-4

Please send comments and questions for Publishing to:
Krystal Lee Enterprises
sales@KLEPub.com

To Reach the Author:
Email: info@IAmMelvina.com

Web: IAMMelvina.com
Contact: Phone: 815-635-8462
Printed in the United States of America.

Disclaimers

The information in this book was correct at the time of publication, but the Author does not assume any liability for loss or damage caused by errors or omissions. These are my memories, from my perspective, and I have tried to represent events as faithfully as possible.

Dedication

For my lover, my best friend, the only man of my life, my husband Glenn
For my three grown daughters, who I love unconditionally and forever will until I die, Mariama, Sierra, and Amira
For my parents who taught me love, gave me love, and I have loved since the beginning of time, Melvin and Albertha
And to any person that believes in yourself, dreams big, works hard, plays harder, and TRULY believes in infinite possibilities and will make it happen, "Come Hell or High Water" …

-This book is for YOU!

Table of Contents

Introduction: I AM Melvina — 7

Chapter One: In the Beginning — 13

Chapter Two: Finding Love — 31

Chapter Three: When Life Heats UP — 43

Chapter Four: Motivation — 63

Chapter Five: What it Takes — 73

Chapter Six: Solid Foundation — 85

Chapter Seven: Dream Big! — 95

Chapter Eight: Starting on the Path — 103

Chapter Nine: Overcoming Challenges — 113

Chapter Ten: Resources — 123

Chapter Eleven: About Melvina Washington — 129

Introduction

Everybody has something to say. It's like body parts; we all have them. What you do with them and how you treat them is to each their own. If you are wondering, as you scan the title, will this book be filled with strong opinions, thoughts, and ideas? To answer your question, I say loudly, "Yes." I am not the woman to bite my tongue, and what I say goes. I set a high standard for myself, and if you set high standards for yourself–or are open to a different approach–I invite you to my world.

> Listen, the consensus is I am still as loud as ever, I can talk to anyone, I am crazy, and I like to laugh. I have never met a stranger in my life. I am simply a down-to-earth Southern type-girl.

Some may think I am too bold, assertive, loud, or opinionated. I can tell you this: assuming I cared about their opinions, I would say they are "picking up

Introduction

what I am putting down, for real," - meaning they are correct. I am very assertive, I know how to speak my mind, I talk loud, and I am bold. The question too many don't care to ask is, "Why?" "Why Melvina, are you so loud?" I have been half-deaf for a very long time. I speak loudly so that I can hear and reassure myself by hearing my own voice.

Do you know how hard it is to be half-deaf in the hood? Do you think people are considerate when they whisper or speak beneath their breath? Do you think every noise piercing the air I hear, or it stirs in me the same response it does for you? It doesn't! I had to learn differently, talk differently, and take a different level of focus for everything I did. I couldn't rely on my senses because some of my challenges prevented me from using them in the same way as others.

I will talk more about my disabilities later in the book, but honestly, that is a conversation all to itself. I never asked someone to feel sorry for me or to throw me a pity party. I learned quickly that having an excuse to fail is not a good enough reason to allow it to happen. Failure is NOT an option for me! Challenges come to everybody, and there are always people who have learned how to win despite their problems and challenges.

I am that person! I refuse to lose, and I do not play to fail. Have I failed upward along the way? Sure, I have. I've been fired before, and I know how it feels. So, when I have had to fire people as a boss, I have no hard feelings whatsoever for my choices. I wasn't raised with a silver spoon in my mouth, and I have a story like everybody else.

I grew up with both my parents in the home, and I enjoyed a nuclear family. Not every day do you meet a strong black family with a child born into marriage; the father and mother remain married, loving each other for over 50 years. But I have that kind of background, and I love it. I make no apologies for how I feel nor for what I have come to realize is true.

If you don't like my boldness and honesty, I am not offended if you close this book right now, but I am going to tell you this: "I am going to give you everything I got to help you win in life. "Come Hell or High Water!" I have been broke, lights cut off, and struggling to make ends meet. I got married over 25 years ago and I am still happily married. I raised a nuclear family of three girls, now adults, just like the one I came from. I lay the law down for my expectations, and everyone around me has to raise the bar!

I wrote this book for women who are ready to be challenged healthily. Who are tired of being told they cannot win by their thoughts, the people they work for, education limitations, or financial constraints. Everything doesn't need money thrown at it. Sometimes, you need to woman up, change your mindset, and fix your position to win! Make no apologies for what must be done to accomplish your purpose and goals.

Get rid of that little girl voice that tells you old sayings, taboos, and projects limitations on your life. I was everything under the sun, but today I am doing things many would have said couldn't be done! I am a

Introduction

business owner and an influencer in my space (Medical Coding). I help families daily, volunteer, raised my children, and am happily married. To have a successful career and marriage makes me unique in this world. What will be your unique factor?

Right now, I want you to commit to casting off every limitation, negative thought, or challenge coming your way. I promise the moment you pick this book up, you will have some challenges thrown at you. There are things in the universe fighting your progress, but overcome the challenges anyway! Don't quit, don't stop, and please kill the excuses.

I do not have time for people's "bitchin' sessions" and complaining about why their lives are not the way they want them to be–and neither should you. I want you to do something most people don't about their problems, work to solve them! For 10, 20, or 30 years we both know people who ain't done nothing but complain, live a neutral life, or stay in the rat race. You have to understand that if you want something and you want it badly enough, you have to work hard and smart to get it.

Having no goals or aspirations and being stuck in neutral with the infamous bitchin' sessions will do nothing and get you nothing! If this is YOU–"LAWD" I pray it is not, keep turning the pages…. If you want something and are okay with working smart, I invite you to turn the page with me.

Melvina W.

Introduction

In the Beginning

Have you ever seen people that you truly admired? I don't mean somebody in a magazine showing you muscles you wish you had, but a good character you know you would like to mimic. I know as women, we think we will identify with our mothers. She is a woman and someday I will be too. You may feel as you see your mother, I want to be just like them. I honestly don't remember saying that growing up exactly–let me be honest. Yes, I grew up with a loving mother who demonstrated she loved us. She was caring and supportive of my father. It seems as if they had an unspoken understanding. Dad lays the foundation, and my mother would support him.

During their marriage, happy to say they still are married, the two of them worked out an understanding and love that stabilized our family. I will always be grateful for their love and willingness to keep the family together. Is it normal in your family like in mind, that children tend to gravitate toward one parent more than another?

In the Beginning

My connection to both of my parents is different. I don't love either one less, but I had a natural closeness with my father. And I couldn't tell you when it formed. If you are honest, your relationship with your father differs from your mother's, right? Come on, speak up; I can't hear you. I remember being little and hanging out with my father. Ironically, my mom and brother also shared most of the time I spent with my father - it was just the 4 of us. But the most memorable times in my life were made up of events, conversations, and laughs with my father specifically.

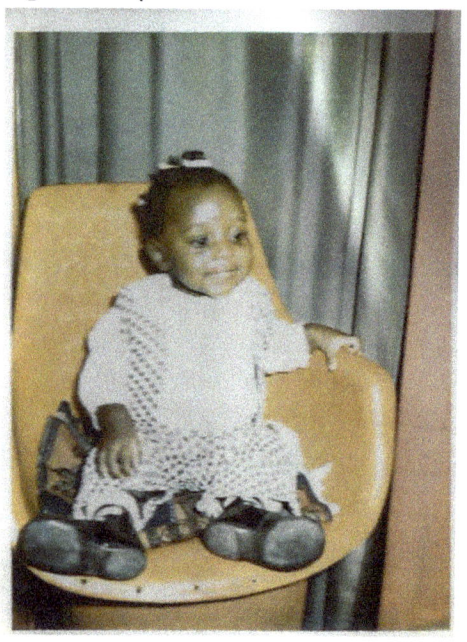

My dad is still as hilarious today as he was when I was a child. I have his funny bone along with some of his other traits. Can I ask you, "What would you do if you were raised by your father and took on his traits more than your mother being a woman?" Do you feel because I act more like my father than my mother, it

Melvina W.

explains why I have a more "dominant" personality? Before you answer that, let me tell you this and circle back to the question.

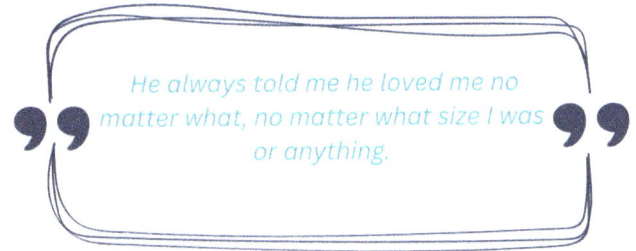

He always told me he loved me no matter what, no matter what size I was or anything.

Again, my dad was fun to hang out with and funny. He could always make me laugh when he told jokes and made faces. I guess that is how he first caught my heart: by making me laugh and helping me to feel important. My father always told me to be the best at everything. He advised me to be better than himself and my mother. He always said, "Marie (he always used my middle name), you can be anything you want to be in this world but you will have to work hard for it."

Another thing I loved about my dad is he had a code of operation known as "Dad's Law." It was an unspoken truth, a fact that didn't need to be said but was widely received. I quickly picked that trait up from my dad, but I super-sized it! I say what I mean, and my thoughts are known throughout the house. I speak my mind and understand that liberty came from my dad.

Every Sunday, we had a church flow. We woke up early, dressed in nice clothes. I got my hair done and spent what felt like three to five hours listening to someone scream and shout as we sat quietly. I did get that message loud and clear from my mother. Neither she nor my father believed in playing around or misbehav-

In the Beginning

ing in church. My mother and father have always been devout believers in Jesus, serving in the church and volunteering their time. Their strong faith was the standard for their marriage; there was no cheating, violence, or bad treatment that we ever saw. The two were a unified front doing everything together in our nuclear family.

My parents would attend functions together for church often. They sometimes attended several church services during the week, visiting the sick and shut-in, praying for people, etc. My church experiences included attending church every Sunday for morning and night services. Prayer services were on Thursdays, choir practice was on Saturdays, and ironically, I sang in the choir two Sundays (1st and 3rd Sundays) every month. Still not done, I also ushered on the usher board on the 2nd Sunday of the month.

It was known that I could not sing, in large part because of my hearing loss, and the choir leader informed me every time I sang the wrong note. I remember when I first joined the "Chancellor Choir," they told me and others who lacked proficiency that they did not want to be embarrassed, so we could not sing in the choir during particular events. I was active within the church mostly due to my parents. The church became essentially my second home, sorry to say!

By the time I reached my teenage years, I rebelled and became an atheist…I was done with the entire Christian belief crap I was hearing for years. That nearly hurt my parents; they were crushed, and then they reiterated the rules of their house - "Everyone goes to church in this house." It wasn't until later when I was 21 years old I realized that I do believe in a higher being or

Melvina W.

God. I realized I am not an atheist or agnostic.

    I respected that my parents are dedicated to the church. The fact they were hard working in every area of their lives didn't shock me either, but I have to say, I did see something wrong with giving all my time throughout the week for churches (volunteering). I was not satisfying my spirit. My soul and the goals or aspirations I had for my life were completely unfulfilled. All of the churches that I have attended were not helping me with my mindset or --- moving me in the right direction to win in business or life.

    Okay, before you throw the Bible at me, let me turn up the heat a bit more. Today, I do not go to church on a regular basis. I do not believe that Jesus is my Lord and Savior, nor do I profess to be a Christian. I know I probably lost a few of you just then, but I have a real reason for how I got there, and I think if you hear me out, we can have an open and honest conversation.

In the Beginning

I am willing to hear the opinions of people who know something, but you cannot come to me with any religious talk or empty actions. This is one thing I do not tolerate, no matter what a person believes, says, or thinks, I am not listening to someone tell me something they themselves don't do. I saw so many hypocrites in churches that they made the streets look sane. Okay, let me get back to my father.

After leaving church service, as a family we would go out for ice cream. Although everyone was present, it felt like my father and I were together alone. He would hold my hand and walk me into the store, and I was in a jolly mood because I knew what I was going to get. I would be thinking about it in church as I bounced my leg up and down while sitting on the pew.

We all would order one by one, and my father would catch the bill. He was a traditional man and believed in paying his way. So we would get our ice cream cones and sit down at the booths. While sitting there with my family, my mother, brother, and father - I found myself looking up, believing that this man really loved me. He wants me to be the best girl I can be. I would ask him after finishing my cone, "Daddy, I want more ice cream. I was good today in church. Can I have it?" He would say, "This girl is always eating up my ice cream and hers," with a hearty chuckle. Without much fight, he would give me more ice cream - strawberry flavor, which I love and still love to this day.

As I licked my ice cream cone and looked at my father, who had worked hard all week, I always thought he was the best father. He would say, I am a hardworking man who can do anything, but make sure you do better than me. " He said, "You might not know what I am talking about now, but one day you will, Marie. Don't you ever forget I told you. Fight hard for what you want, Marie."

I quickly replied as I ate my ice cream, "But Daddy, life is so good. What more could I want?" I remember saying that back to him because, at the time, I didn't know what more I could want out of life. We weren't rich but far from poor. We had a house that my parents worked hard to get and maintain. They made sure to give us stability, so my struggles didn't start until I was an adult. My father and I had many more conversations like this one when I was very young. However, I listened to him but didn't fully understand him.

> Listen, the consensus is I am still as loud as ever, I can talk to anyone, I am crazy, and I like to laugh. I have never met a stranger in my life. I am simply a down-to-earth Southern type-girl.

But there was a switch within him that once clicked, he became a strong disciplinarian and enforced his rules, or "Dad's Law." Not in a bad way, but my father was a balanced man. For all the encouragement he gave me, he also anchored me with discipline. In addition, my dad did not have a college education. He dropped out of high school, so his reading and comprehension of reading materials were extremely limited as an adult. Where my father may have been weak in reading, he made up for it by being extremely visual.

In the Beginning

To overcompensate for the lack of reading and understanding things, he could watch something done or performed and remember it well enough to replicate it - this is how he excelled. He was always a resourceful leader who found a way to win. Good leaders must have this component: a strong desire to win Come Hell or High Water, naturally, regardless of challenges.

He would give no excuses for why he didn't get something we needed. His ability to set a standard that kept everyone's best interest at heart was something I adopted. In my home, I do have Melvina's Law, and that same law goes for my business and relationships. I am quick to say I don't know everything, but what I do know, I will not let anyone shut me down or put me into a box. While I am my father's daughter, I have his visual learning skill set, but I can also read, write, and comprehend material on a college level. Essentially, I took something from my father's drive, and it motivated me to embrace visual learning, being hardworking with a strong work ethic, and expanding it.

Nobody ever told me I was supposed to admire my dad and act like my mother. So, I chose to love my mom and act like my dad.

I may be a woman, but I am the best part of my father's character. His sense of humor and playfulness I employ even today. At the same time, I employ his drive, motivation and born-leader skills too. I am my father's legacy - I took what he had to give with his wisdom, and I multiplied it by 100 by becoming educated, an entrepreneur, mother, wife, and blah, blah.

I remember one day, as we sat around the dinner table, I asked my parents why they were working so hard. My momma had a job down at the church as a custodian, and my daddy worked at Great Dane Trailers for ten hours or more a day. They both were hustlers and willing to work to add value to the family. Collectively, they both worked for the local Penny Saver (a local newspaper and advertisement paper) and cleaned a second or sometimes third church weekly.

They both seemed to have 5 jobs at any given time, with mom also working to clean an office weekly and my dad working odd jobs like helping people move and fixing and painting cars, among other side jobs. On that day, I said to both of them in a light-hearted but serious way, "All the time y'all work and have like 5 jobs to make ends meet. I don't want to be like y'all when I grow up," I told them as the four of us sat and had dinner at the kitchen table.

I continued, "I want a maid so I do not have to do house cleaning. I will NOT have 50 million jobs like you all." My parents laughed at me and told me that they would be my maid. And my father's infamous words were, "Marie, keep living, just keep living."

I remember one day, my father came home completely exhausted. At this time I was a teenager seeing him follow a habitual pattern of hard work. He worked himself to the bone, and that was a familiar song and dance I saw each night. On this day, however, it felt different. He came into the house as I was sitting in the living room. He shuffled over toward the coach but

In the Beginning

plopped down into his favorite chair. With eyes barely open as he leans back in the recliner, he says, "Marie, do better than me. Don't live like us. I want you to be better than me and momma."

I instantly recalled the conversation years prior when I said I wanted a maid and not to have to work a million jobs. My mom's response after she laughed and my dad joked was, "You gonna get a maid, huh?" I confidently responded, "Yes, and I will pay them $400 a week." Right then, I knew something was different. I think differently than my mother and father. Today, my mom jokes and says, "Got dang it she said what she wanted at 11 years old and went out and did it." Essentially, today, I have a maid who helps me out a few times a week, and yes, I pay her $400 a week. I am smiling when I say that.

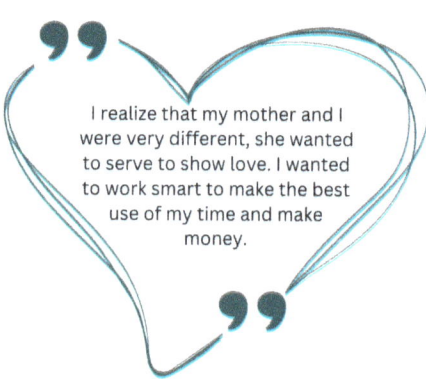

I realize that my mother and I were very different, she wanted to serve to show love. I wanted to work smart to make the best use of my time and make money.

My parents and I had numerous conversations, but this one hit really "made some noise" in my slang terms. I reflect on how this conversation and his words sparked questions. I started to look at how my parents lived, survived, and provided for our family. They did a great job with keeping us above water but I questioned, was this the only way or the best way, and will I choose the same? I was always a go-getter, but this statement made me realize working and getting a job wasn't enough. My dad had three jobs, and my mother worked, yet all this working didn't mean we had everything we could have had.

Although we occasionally had some tight financial situations, with more bills seeming to come in than money, we managed to have family vacations. Our vacations were on a very "low " economic scale. You know, those budget trips where everyone stayed in one hotel room, slept on the floor if needed, cooked on a hot plate, and bought groceries to cook instead of eating out. We never flew anywhere but would only drive. If the hotel and vacation could not be done on the east coastline, we were not going. Often, our trips were for visiting family and not recreational fun.

It was a struggle, I know, to keep our house, and I figured that was in large part because my parents were not college graduates. They didn't work smart but very hard, once I figured that out, I affixed my mind on a goal that was unmovable. My parents didn't take the time to pursue an education beyond grade school. I didn't want that for myself or my children. I made it a standard not to consider myself educated until I earned at least my bachelor's degree.

I loved my mother, but I didn't see myself in her growing up. We disagreed more than I care to rehash, and most of our differences were about my mindset. I remember asking her a series of questions growing up that she was kind enough to answer honestly without my probing thoughts being seen as "fighting words." I started the interview that helped shape my mindset and built characteristics in me similar to my mother's.

I remember asking her: "Mom, why are you fixing dinner for all of us? All the time, you are clean-

In the Beginning

ing, fixing dinner, and doing laundry. Do you like doing all this stuff?" She thought about what I said for a brief moment and replied, "Well, Marie, your father works so hard, the least I can do is have a warm cooked meal for him when he comes home." Her response was not complicated, and even as a child, I could understand the need to service those I cared about. BUT I replied, "I understand it needs to be done, but why do you have to do it? Why do you meal prep, cook, and take care of Dad?"

"You even have my brother and I cleaning and tossing out the trash. Why do we have to clean the house? Why does my brother take out the trash every week and do the yard work? Why do we have to do these duties?" I don't think she understood my perspective of what I was really asking or my mindset even then as a child. I could understand the need for things needing to be done, but why did the action have to be completed by us? Couldn't we hire help or do things differently?

At that moment, I realized I didn't have the traditional mindset that women were to be domestic cleaners, fashioning their lives to support their husbands and organizing the children to do the same. I received the lesson of family support, but I wanted more than to bury myself in house chores, I wanted to chase my dreams and accomplish them. Throughout the years, I remember asking her, "Did you ever want to be anything else career-wise growing up?" She stated, "Well, I wish I would have taken up cashiering as a trade cause then I could have moved up from there."

My mother expressed her ambitions for cashiering through her skill set in bookkeeping and helping the family stay afloat. She didn't see how to monetize her interest and gifts beyond working with her hands in a domestic capacity. This doesn't take anything away from my mother's heart. She is a woman that enjoys serving others, she will even do the grunt work to express her love. However, I determined a long time ago if I don't have to do grunt work, I will gladly pay a landscaper, groundskeeper, maid, or anyone else who can help give me time to pursue my own interests. I was determined to live my dreams and be fairly compensated for it without apology.

I think if I were a male child, she wouldn't have cared about my mindset so much–but I wasn't. She wanted me to be her little mini-me, but instead, I was my father, trapped in a girl's body. I was loud, opinionated, a born-leader, and couldn't wait to get a maid growing up. I just felt that women had more to give than domestic work and support for their husband's ambitions.

My mother maintained a traditional female role that I could not accept as my life's purpose. This was another problem I had with the church, they had set gender roles they forced on people and did not take into account people's personalities. I was not a submissive woman in the respect I would have to be silent and listen to my husband. I wasn't built like that at all, and my mother was very different. I started wanting things that my family either didn't care to have or were too busy working to go and obtain.

My father worked hard, but I didn't see him

In the Beginning

work smart. He warned me about it, and I frequently observed my life through that lens. Do I want to work my hands and body to the bone and never travel to Europe, Asia, or my favorite Africa? Places we learned about in school, I wanted to see and touch with my hands. Could I fully embrace who I was, a leader with a mindset to obtain the things I dreamed about? Or would I have to settle for being happy with loving my family and children. I honestly felt I should have never had to decide between the two- the two were linked to making money that made both possible.

I questioned why, as I looked at my mother she didn't chase her dreams to be the cashier she had dreamt of becoming. She could have made more money, got more time to spend with us, and perhaps lived a life – to me of greater importance. But my mother was not me, and she found enjoyment in living life as she chose to. Yes, she stayed in the house, worked cleaning other people's offices and businesses, and helped to raise her children–which are all wonderful things, but I didn't want this same fate.

" Be careful how you judge your parents because someday, the same questions can present themselves to you. "

I wanted to love my mother like she deserved, but I struggled to show that because of some of her ways I rejected. I know I hurt her feelings, writing this even today may hurt her feelings, but that is not my intention. Sometimes, we have to stand up for what we want

Melvina W.

in life. My dad nursed a voice in me, and by the time I was a teenager, my mindset and voice were set.

My mom and I didn't see eye to eye on domestic matters, but she did contribute a considerable amount to my life. My mother took the time to help stabilize my confidence growing up. She would tell me when I was bullied or made fun of for being dark in complexion, "Don't dwell on things like your weight. You are beautiful and if people don't see that, they are the stupid ones." Because of that constant reassurance, thinking about my weight doesn't change my impression of myself or make me believe I deserve anything less than what I demand.

My mother was one of the first to hear and see

In the Beginning

my logic play out. She didn't like it, but she grew to respect it. She allows me to be a "daddy's girl" and will call on my father's help to weigh in on conversations where we don't agree. Only we agreed on how to show love through acts of service, the way we showed our love varied considerably. I did not want my future to be hedged on the skills or mindset of a man. I wanted to have more say on if I lived a life of luxury or poverty. My father always told me, "Be the best you can be, Marie." No matter what I choose to do in life, I choose to do it to the best of my ability. I took that to heart and then some!

Be careful how you judge your parents because someday, the same questions can present themselves to you.

My mom did teach me invaluable tips on life, like how to mother and the value of marriage and family. I have always had a strong conviction that women who desire to marry should create a nuclear family if at all possible. My mom was strict in that she strongly disapproved of us being irresponsible. My mother was always nurturing and caring, and she always made the house a home. My mother would say, "Dress like a lady, look like a lady, and respect yourself."

She always told me that "Black is beautiful." In

my teenage years, I was teased very badly for being so dark-skinned in the 70's and 80's. She always believed that I should be educated but not on the same level I believed - she stressed a trade school… Here, my father agreed we couldn't have any babies in their house, and we didn't. She told me I could and should do well in school and in general to make her and my father proud. She got used to us not being alike, although she never accepted my different mindset as the best.

This is a matter of opinion, and I am not ashamed one bit that the two of us can love each other but not agree. I can never be like my mother, so I can respect her if she doesn't want to be me. I often wonder, what is there not to like about me? Can anyone say that my life is not amazing? Did I not make my parents proud by achieving great success, having a nuclear family, and managing a household while getting 4 degrees?

I worked very hard to get to where I am in life, and I don't regret the sacrifices I had to make. Some would call me aggressive, too bold, arrogant, or selfish. But I will tell you right now, everything I've done, I did for love, family and money. Making money, love and family are the three most important factors in my life. They move and motivate me. Did I get everything right, no, but I have a lot to show for my journey, and I can help you do the same.

The words of my father echoed in my head and the encouragement from my mother that I was good enough. Whenever I hear people tell me, "No, Melvina, that cannot be done." Or, no, the Bible says this about that. The church says this or that. I would hear my parents' words. Am I a person who doesn't believe in God

In the Beginning
Almighty, no. I believe in God, I just don't believe that God needs man to do anything."

God is all-powerful, why would He need people? He may want us to do things, but at the same time, he doesn't make us. He gives us free choice, and I choose to say yes to the things I dream about. As long as I am not hurting anybody breaking the law, I am going to find a way to get a "yes." I made goals that I wasn't sure how I would accomplish, but by faith knew it would happen.

I remember when I got married and we gave birth to our first child. When I was sitting in the dark because our lights were shut off from nonpayment, I said I was traveling to Africa first class. I vowed not to live like that anymore but to afford us better. Who knew I could see that far into my future even if the lights were out! I wasn't looking at what I saw, I was looking at what is possible. We all need to look at what is possible, not based on what we've seen, had, or our parents have accomplished–but what is available.

I can tell you, if I never thought about going to Africa, who's to say I would have ever made provision to go? I know some of you are trailblazers out here doing things that have never been done in your families. For some of us, breaking the mold is taking vacations, starting a business, or shifting our financial expectations. I have been to Ghana, Togo, the United Kingdom, France, Italy, Turkey and many more countries because I made a plan to go.

Dreaming alone is not enough, you have to put action into play. An action plan is always work, and if you work, in the beginning, you may work the hardest.

Melvina W.

Experience is not something you are given but earned. In every job I had, I used whatever resources I could to point me in the direction of getting what I wanted for myself and my family. You are going to hear me repeat my three motivators throughout the book, but I want each time you read it for it to bring you also back to your WHY or your goals.

It is normal to ponder if you are faced with the same choices as your parents, would you make the same decisions. Entering my next phase of life, I was met with the demands of family, school, and business. I had to watch myself to see if I would become my mother or fully embrace being Melvina, even if that meant I stood against the constructs of typical gender roles to get there!

In the Beginning

Finding Love

Nobody intends on living life by their lonesome. We all have an idea for someone to be around us, cheering us on or living life with us. Stepping out on my own and choosing to live life was challenging. I have never lied to my girls and told them life would be easy. I will stand on my position, "You have to work hard because dreaming doesn't make it happen."

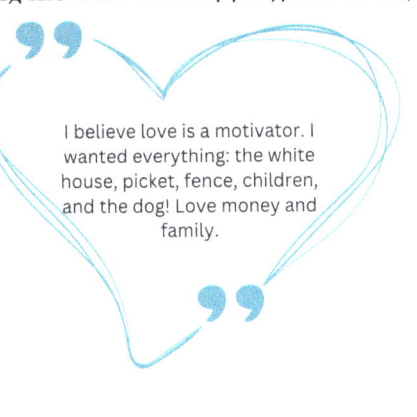

I believe love is a motivator. I wanted everything: the white house, picket, fence, children, and the dog! Love money and family.

This doesn't just apply to work ethic but also in life and relationships. I have never been a woman who was careless with my mind, body, soul or spirit. I am guarded although I am open, you see. Listen, the consensus is I am loud, can talk to anyone, I've been called

Finding Love

crazy, and I love to laugh. I never met a stranger in my life. I am a down-to-earth Southern type of girl. Being a risk-taker and go-getter makes me bold and adventurous.

I was ready to leave home and live life on my terms. My parents set me up for life in that I knew how to cook, clean, keep a house, and work hard. When I set out on my own, I knew the value of working to get money. I quickly saw that working smart was the only way to amass money as quickly as I needed it.

Looking to see who was hiring wasn't my goal, I looked to see what was hiring and could pay what I needed. After searching papers, talking to people, and getting details on money-making jobs through the grapevine, getting into hospitality made sense. My dynamic character and gift of gab made me a shoo-in to serve.

Not all restaurants or bars are created equal. The clientele greatly determined how much money I could make, and I didn't want any broke folks. If you want to attract money, you have to be around people who spend. I had no interest in dancing or joining in on the club scene, but I saw how much money circled around in nightclubs.

I learned how to say what I needed to, making people comfortable and open to spending and enjoying themselves. I don't have to do "something strange for some change," but I just have to learn from people. We can underestimate how helpful it is to have an ideal personality. The reality is people buy you long before they see the product or service. The way you look, talk and present a brand does impact whether people buy or not.

I lived so fat off my tips and made so much money that I was able to buy my first house on my serving salary. Working at Club 112, I knew was temporary, so I wanted to use my employment, connections, and money to work for me. Many of you work jobs that pay good money.

I am motivated by three fundamental things: love, family, and money. I had money but didn't have love or family in my life. I wanted to round out what I valued most, so dating was something that came as a natural progression. I am a picky person, and I would be quick to admit that. Meeting my first husband wasn't a whole lot to talk about. We met, fell in love, and tried to make it work, it didn't, so we both moved on.

The best thing I can say about that marriage, I had no children with him. Our break was clean and fast. I never thought about checking up on him or seeing how his life turned out. I believe when things are done, let them end. I wanted a nuclear family and I did thank God I had a chance to achieve it.

I wasn't on the hunt for a quick replacement, but the right one. I remember dating Otis. This, too, will be a quick conversation. I met Otis when in college. I was making money and I had a mindset that we can build together. Only, Otis was a handsome guy but not ambitious enough for me. I tried to be patient, we dated for almost a year before I called it quits.

He was okay with meeting and going to dinner. I felt he half listened to me and didn't pay attention. If he were, he would have known he was born with a quick fuse. But to be fair, he also felt the separation between the two of us.

I remember one time he and I attended a family house party or get together at a friend's house. At the party, he seemed distant, but I didn't pay it much mind because I was checking out anyhow. He was having group conversations and telling everyone we were "just friends" and not dating.

At the school or either at the house party was this Computer "playing video games" geek, Glenn, who asked Otis, "Hey, who's that?" Glenn listened to every word Otis said. But he wanted to be sure there would be no issues with Otis about his intentions, so he asked again on a different day, "Hey man, what's up with you and Marie?" Otis said again, "Naw, we are just friends." Glenn nodded his head and I believe at that moment he made plans for me.

You see, Glenn had a thing for dark chocolate. The darker, the better, and I was it. He came up to me and introduced himself. He was kind, funny, and kept things brief. After seeing him at the house party, ironically, I saw him more and more at school. Just like when you pick your dream car, and it keeps popping up, that was how I felt with him. We both were enrolled at DeVry University and majoring in Computer Information Systems.

Yes, a Geek love triangle may have you swooning, but it was not full of drama like the movies. Otis and I soon after the party split. Glenn and I started studying together and talking about computers. It has always been easy to talk with him. He was such a gentleman, and our conversations never got intimate.

To get what you want, you have to understand the value of taking things slow. Don't be quick to rush in and get the prize, but work to get to know someone and what you want. Getting to know Glenn was one of the best decisions of my life. After parting from Otis, he was a breath of fresh air. Naturally, Glenn and I grew closer.

I remember one day we were watching TV at my house. His coming over was no big deal, this was our norm, in fact. In sunny Georgia, he knocked at the door. Unassuming, I answered the door with a bowl of popcorn already popped! We loved to eat snacks, talk about people in movies, and laugh a lot. One of the best things to do for a good time is to watch people. I don't have a lot of time, but I recall waiting on planes at the airport and eating at the mall. As I sat, I watched the people going by and just laughed.

Glenn and I had an instant connection, and it grew deeper over the months that we were friends. He truly was my best friend. As we watched the TV and joked, I remember him mushing me on the side of my head. If you are familiar, that means he gave me a gentle nudge. Of course, my dad didn't raise a punk, so even when playing, I was tagging you back.

When I sense I can't win, I get resourceful. I spotted a pillow I knew was packed with foam, and I swang. "Bop!" It hit him in the head and landed. He said, "Oh so we pillow fighting now?" He picked up another pillow and gently swung in my direction. He missed, and I started laughing. "I pray that is not all you got, shame, shame," I said playfully. He laughed and said, "Alright, forget this pillow.

He turned to me, came up close, and gave me a bear hug. I dropped the pillow, and we both landed on the couch. We have play-wrestled before and had pillow fights, but this time he ended up landing on top of me. I joked and said, "What? Do you like me or something?" He said sincerely, looking into my eyes, "Yes, I do."

Our connection grew, and fast forward to about 2 months into our relationship, Otis caught wind that we were dating. It was not known to me at this time, he told all his friends we were "just friends." When Glenn told me one day, I was surprised, but I shouldn't have been. What surprised me was his reaching out to tell me he wanted to give us another shot.

I almost laughed when I read the letter Glenn left on my car 27 years ago, that was our version of texting. If Glenn had questionable character, I might have questioned if he lied to me about what Otis said, but there was no slick behavior he ever showed me. He was a genuine man, and I loved that about him. I phoned a close friend, Tonya at the time like I was on a game show or something and let her know what was happening. I remember, Tonya said, "You ain't heard from Otis in what 6 months? Why not give the new guy a chance? You already know what Otis is all about."

Now, to be honest, with a name like Otis, he just sounds old when I think about it, and all his talking was "old" and tired! I agreed with her wholeheartedly, and Glenn and I kept dating. You see, when the good comes into your life, you cannot return to the old things you used to do, date, or what you've had. I am not the biggest technology person, but I understand the value of having new gadgets compared to dated equipment. I know sometimes, to fix something costs more than starting off fresh.

To fix the relationship with Otis would have cost way more than I cared to spend in time. Plus, Otis didn't have the money to pay for anything. I wanted a partnership, and this country boy didn't have it. I didn't want to pull his weight when he was giving me nothing in return. Don't feel guilty when you terminate relationships or job opportunities. If you have a direction, a plan, and somewhere you need to be. If where you are is not getting you there or functioning as a stepping stool, get on.

Glenn and I connected, and I was making a steady income the entire time. I was determined to get my money working and I decided to buy a house. I didn't want a man to rob me of this accomplishment, and I am glad he didn't fight me on it. I wanted to buy this house in my name and prove to myself a man didn't make me or secure my living; I did! It was a great accomplishment to buy my first house, but I didn't want to experience it alone. I wanted a family.

Having a roommate when you first leave home I strongly suggest if you want to move up fast. I would apply this rule to anything in your life. It is better to move with help and support than to wing it alone. During our lease agreement, I was completely in my element and had no restraints. I wanted to keep this life.

Moving day came, and Glenn and I were so

happy. He celebrated me and never attempted to dwindle my confidence. To make me feel even more secure, he moved in with me. At the age of 24, I bought my first house with a service attendant salary. Homeownership is not as complicated as people think. It does take patience and managing money well to make the process go smoothly. After a month or two of living in peace, Glenn and I got pregnant with our first baby girl.

We were so happy, and Glenn showed me so much love and attention. My pregnancy went by quickly, and it felt like, before we knew it, she was here. It was such a life adjustment to go from attending college for a few years, partying, and working to meeting the love of my life in 1995. We welcomed the arrival of our daughter in 1996 but didn't marry until 1998.

If you know like I do, you want to be sure. Don't allow a baby to be the reason you marry someone if it is not right. Likewise, don't go making babies with a man you see no future with. That is an unnecessary roadblock. Those first 2 years were a struggle. I made more than Glenn, and when my income dwindled the idea of being a stay at home mom, taking care of the children, started to quickly dissipate. We needed money, and we needed it fast!

What I didn't tell you, I dropped out of school when pregnant with baby number one. I had to spend more time working and I couldn't juggle work, school, a husband, and a new baby; something had to give. I was grateful we had already purchased our house because that was a good push forward. Just when we thought the storm was calming, we found out we were pregnant with twin girls. Now in 2000, 3 girls all under 6 was a challenge.

Oh my, I didn't know what was coming for me when suddenly… life happened. Life gave me a big kick in the butt as I felt the uneasiness of bills coming one after the other. Bills are not a problem when you have the money, but they were a pain when there was not enough money coming in from our checks to pay the bills. We used to have to "rob Peter to pay Paul," essentially. Then, one day we were watching TV and the lights got disconnected.

I thought that the electricity was down for the entire neighborhood; so I walked outside to check out what had happened. It was then I realized it was just our house that didn't have power. I had to float a check because payday wasn't for another week. This was one of the rock bottom moments for me. The others are too embarrassing to tell…OMG!! (oh my goodness, honey).

The house was pitch black that night and I had nothing but time to think. I needed to quit the house and settle my mind to get serious about the dreams I had planned many years ago. It wasn't all in a day that I turned the corner. Unfortunately, after several more embarrassing moments, I knew what kind of life I wanted to live. I did not just want to survive. I want to have financial freedom and be debt-free. I decided I had to make myself successful – no matter what!

When life is difficult, it is at these times we need to reflect on what we have accomplished. Buying the house was such a confidence booster, along with having love, and family. I just needed to add money to the picture. I went back to an idea and a fundamental flaw

Finding Love
of my parents, I needed more education.

Working with your hands is not smart if you are trading laborious work for payment. Working hourly, especially for minimum wage is not the answer. I am not sure who is supposed to live off of that, but I had to go back to the basics and finish my education. Going to school wasn't a walk in the park and the decision did not instantly change my living circumstances.

I know we feel that when we make the right decision to move forward, the effects will be immediately realized and felt. I was struggling to complete my Associate's degree in 2000. Can you imagine birthing twins and going to school, all while floating checks to pay my bills, borrowing from friends (the old money swap, because they were broke too), taking out payday loans, etc?

It got ugly before it got better, I will be honest. If you thought I took a break, wrong, I pushed through to get my bachelor's degree in 2002. I told myself there was nothing to celebrate until I got my bachelor's. When I earned that degree, money was still funny. I quickly realized a bachelors was an incredible accomplishment but it wasn't enough for me–not for what I planned. So, I enrolled in my master's program and graduated in 2005; but while I was attending, I also went to a medical coding boot camp and got my coding certification.

What I was doing was not easy, let me tell you. If you think getting to where you want to be is going to fall into your lap, you are "smoking crack." I mean, you smoked the complete rock and reached for another. In case you are unfamiliar, being accused of smoking crack

Melvina W.

means you are not thinking things through coming from Melvina. If you feel overwhelmed at times and think of quitting, I did, too, but let me tell you what we will miss out on if we quit at the beginning of the story.

Now turn with me to chapter three…

Finding Love

When Life Heats UP

Life knows how to cook up pressure. In your life, your tests and trials are needed to help push you. If you are right now feeling overwhelmed, just breathe and get ready to get on. We all have problems, challenges, and issues, but that is not an excuse to fail. I want to add my road to getting to where I am now in no capacity, as you can see, already came easy.

Keep in mind that I got three degrees while having babies, getting married, and buying a house. I had to learn to juggle bills and hustle to finish school. I did everything I knew to do with the time I had to progress my life. If you are reading this book and saying, I can't do this. Stop it. You can do this, and if you don't, you will be in the same place you have been. It is time to woman up, girly, and get this done!

Your dreams and accomplishing your goals are your responsibility. No one owes you a thing, and the quicker you get that, the happier you will become. Not allowing others to dictate your happiness but finding that from within is the first mindset test you need to hone in on. I have so much more to say on the topic but I am going to sprinkle some in each chapter for sure.

What I want to focus on right now is my family dynamics and how they changed over the years. After putting in years of hard work and going to school non-stop, I couldn't get a job. We all know about this unspoken hidden catch twenty-two, if you don't have experience you won't get the job. How can I get a job to learn and prove my skills if no one is willing to take a chance on me?

I was frustrated, but I didn't spend all this time and money to give up because my resume was getting shut down sight unseen because of my lack of experience. They didn't care that I passed all my classes with the highest and best scores. It irked me for sure, like I am sure it does for you when you know you are the best and apply yourself, but others won't see past their misconceptions of you.

My husband was very supportive of me and launched my career. While I was studying and he was the God sent I needed to manage our home. I am an ambitious person. My husband is less ambitious than me. He is like the tortoise and I am the hare. I am in a hurry to get on with the program, where my husband would choose the slow and steady route. Sometimes, he makes me feel he is not moving, but for my accomplishments, he has accomplished just as much but on a different scale.

We have both purchased homes ourselves. I did it faster, but he got it done. I finished multiple degrees, but he has some certifications. I make my salary, and he makes his. We are both doing very well financially, so money is not why we choose to stay together. We honestly love each other.

I remember when I got my first real job in 2006 after working short contracts and gigs for a few years. The job was a huge commitment for my family because it required the whole family to move to Jacksonville. My husband's flexible nature permitted his confidence to move for my career. I don't know about you, but not too many men move for their wives' careers. Do you know one or many with that kind of story?

But this job earned me an income of 75k a year and I was so proud. Even though we had more money coming in, we also had bigger expenses. We had two houses; one that we were renting in Jacksonville and two paying off the mortgage in Georgia. Life was no picnic at all these days, I was working my butt off at the job to prove and learn my skill. The long nights and overtime did weigh on my marriage, and arguments swirled under the pressure.

Glenn and I have always maintained the principle of not going to bed angry with each other. Glenn is not straightforward and direct like I am. I have to pull things out of him because he is shy and reserved. There were some long talks we had that kept me up at night, amongst other activities, if you know what I mean, and I would have to wake up to work overtime the next day. Even though I had a job paying that kind of money, it wasn't enough. We needed more, my family needed more.

I was very honest about what motivates me, love,

When Life Heats UP

family, and money. I know there are some assumptions that if women like money, they are gold diggers, heartless, or ruthless. I want to show you that this is a misconception. Everyone needs motivation–no matter what it is to drive them to achieve their optimum potential. For some of us, it is money, for others love, children, progress, achievement, accolades, etc.

I don't care what needs to be in view for you to want to fight but get your fight. Life is going to send hell your way, and you must have the power to counter it. I had to dig deep because on the days I wanted to fall asleep, and struggled on the job, got reprimanded, I couldn't cry my eyes out and quit. I had to fight, and your fight begins in your mind.

When things got tough, I had to remember what was important to me, love, family, and money. Love has always been first for me. So, when my husband struggled with my schedule and my girls, it weighed on me, too. My top two priorities were being challenged, and I wasn't making enough money. I wasn't miserable but also wasn't happy.

We worked this challenging schedule for a few years before moving back to Georgia. Paying two house payments and dealing with deadbeat renters who tore up our house forced us to decide between the two states. Will we decide to buy in Jacksonville and sell our Georgia house or vice versa? Without hesitation, we chose to move back to Georgia.

Moving back was the best option out of the two, but it was also not easy. We had to move into a house that had drywall missing, these people literally punched holes in walls, ruined the carpet, and damaged the cabinets. Every appliance in the house had to be removed and replaced. I was as mad as a bull chasing a red flag blowing in my face.

When you are angry that power is best harvested and focused towards your goals, rather than bitchin' and complaining. This is one of the moments Glenn held me as I walked through my house and felt the loss of my investment property, money and all. So, I know what it means to work very hard and invest your money and someone else takes it away. Being that hurt, I never again want to experience that kind of loss of that magnitude.

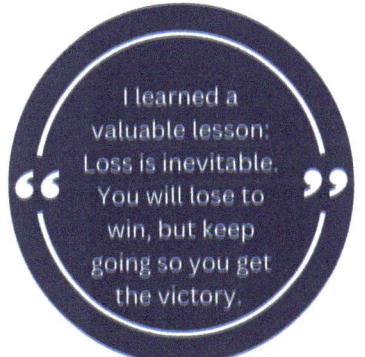

> I learned a valuable lesson: Loss is inevitable. You will lose to win, but keep going so you get the victory.

Glenn and I work together because we both bring something different to the table. We don't have traditional gender roles some would argue, but our connection works. When I moved back, I worked a few odd-end jobs before landing a traveling position in Houston. I had to fly out and return weekly. My husband was the only reason I felt comfortable taking the job that changed our lives. He didn't have to lead our family with his career, I never needed him to do that because I have always been a woman that can lead.

" He is my man, and I am going to stay with him. He works for me. The marriage works. When you have people on your team, don't drop them because they don't fit someone's preference. Focus on your needs."

When Life Heats UP

In a strong marriage, you can operate as a unit even if the two of you are not in the same state or place. We were looking for a break to happen in our finances– and it did, but it meant me leaving home weekly. I never thought I would have to be a helicopter mom, dropping down here and there and teaching from phones and computers. It might sound like a lot of fun to travel every week, stay in hotels, have roommates, and drive rental cars the company pays for, but it was hard on my family.

As much as I love making money, I fully enjoy being a mother and a wife. My mom taught me the valuable lesson of being nurturing, caring, and supportive of my children. I saw all of them take their first steps, was around when they grew their first tooth, and I didn't miss them saying their first word.

These are moments that melted my heart, and when I traveled, I missed them intensely. My goal was to provide my children with what I never had. I knew it would take hard work, but I didn't think accomplishing this goal meant leaving home. This arrangement both-

Melvina W.

ered me because I strongly believed in being a mother who was very involved in my children's lives and being there for them in all aspects of life - from birth until I die…because I am their mother, NOT their friend, home girl, or anything like that…

I am the type of mother that is nurturing, caring, and supportive (within reason because I am NOT gonna support any and everything that they want), but I have never deprived them of what they need and deserve. I have and will always encourage my children to be the best because that is the standard. I know the importance of raising daughters with strong character, by giving them the belief system that they can and they will get an education. They will know how to live and win in life single or married.

I am extremely communicative with them and a disciplinary type of mother. I guess I got that from my father, also. I do not run a democracy. I will state the rules of the house and expect them to be followed because I set examples of what a lady should look like, act like, and think like. We are not raising damsels in distress or women ignorant of life circumstances. It burned a pain in my heart when my eldest daughter started her menstruation, and I was away.

> As a parent, I made every effort to be present and an equal partner in raising our girls.

My husband was a trooper and dealt with it as best as he could, and as soon as I got there that week-end, I helped address the situation. I didn't want to be behind the eight ball with our twins and I knew other conversations and supervision were needed when talking about boys, sex, and other delicate stuff. My husband could not do it alone. It was time for me to start looking at life in a very different way that freed up my time and allowed me to maximize my income.

> As a parent, I made every effort to be present and an equal partner in raising our girls.

I am a fair mom but wouldn't say I am easy. I have had several rules that I expected everyone to follow. I respected my girls and demanded they do the same for me and their father. When they were children the expectation was they would follow the rules of the house, do their chores, clean their room, clean up behind themselves, do their homework, etc. We had a strong stance on education, and I often said, "YOU WILL complete school no matter what. College is not optional. NO Matter what…I wasn't compromising on this issue."

I saw first hand what a lack of education can do, and the number one thing was it removed options. So, it was implanted into my children's brains that NO babies come into this house unless I make them with their Father… NOPE! You've heard of the saying "poster child," well I am the poster parent of one that will put you out with the baby. It is not the baby I am against, but the circumstances. I don't think it is fair for my girls to bring a child into the world without being responsible for them.

To best afford a child and have the mental capac-

Melvina W.

ity to manage a home–while being married, they had to finish college. I struggle with attending college after having a child and getting married. I wanted them to get it right on the first try and not fumble around in the dark. And no, I wasn't trying to pay for a college degree in acting, that could be an elective, but it is not a VERY lucrative degree. I want real discipline and would happily write the check. My youngest daughter (Amira) wanted to go to school for hair...I affectionately said, "NOPE," and then she said, "What about film or theater?" My answer again was NOPE!"

If they were adamant about going in a different direction than I had advised, they could do it, and I wouldn't stop them. BUT, they would have to leave the very GOOD setup I built, cell phone, car, own bedroom, etc to go and pave their own way. They can make me a believer, but if not, it is best to follow a map that has already been proven to lead to treasure.

When Life Heats UP

I can feel some of you right now judging this decision of mine, but today, I have three daughters that have COMPLETED college, all of whom have their own places, pay their bills, and are responsible adults. None of them had babies in high school, and they all are still without children. If they want a different lifestyle or orientation they could not explore that either in my house. Their father and I knew what was best to keep them safe and we did that. May have not been perfect but my children did not miss out on a thing.

Every year, they enjoyed Christmas and family vacations. I have gone all out for them, buying things they asked for and needed. If they needed something for school or for life like cell phones, cars, school supplies, clothes, etc, they had it. I remember when each of our girls turned 16, I bought them a car cash from a used car lot. I wasn't crazy and bought them new cars. You know teenagers are going to ding up a car, and if they want luxury, they are going to work for it and spend their own money.

Glenn may think I did the most when raising our daughters, but I wanted them to know what they deserved. Flying first class, yes, they should experience it. I set my sights on traveling to Africa–and with my entire family YES we did it. It was one of the best family trips we had taken.

When we went to Europe, I wasn't planning on visiting one country, England. I wanted us to go to Paris also. When would be a better time to backpack through Europe other than now, when I am here? Who knows when we would have time to get back because I never thought money would be the reason. I wanted a lifestyle, and when I determined I deserved it, I never shifted from that concept.

I remember Glenn and I got into an argument about going to Paris. He thought we should have stayed in London and enjoyed the sights. Nothing wrong with that, but I had it in my mind to sit at one of those fancy Bistro places and have a fancy drink in my hand. I didn't know what the drink would be. I don't drink coffee or tea, but I wanted to experience it. I work hard and I play even harder, and yes, I enjoy the fruits of my labor. I told Glenn, "We are going to Paris. If you don't want to go, you can stay here, but we are going."

Glenn hesitated, but he wound up having a great time–we all did. It was another vacation that proved

When Life Heats UP

Mom's way is the best way. I am not always right, and Glenn surely brings something to the table. I move quickly, and Glenn moves slower than I do. Maybe he has more patience than me, I could argue, but I never tried to change that about him. My parenting style and Glenn's as I said were different but we had an understanding.

> I gave you a pretty good IDEA..and NO, it has NOT been peaches and cream around here!! No ma'am!!

Glenn as a father...

Glenn didn't have the same advantage I had of having his father in the home. He grew up in a single-family household, and all of his siblings were boys. Growing up in a house full of boys, perhaps would explain why he didn't talk much–he was around his brothers, and the only woman in the house was his mother. But Glenn is a gentleman and a man you wouldn't mind for your daughter to bring home and meet the family.

In the beginning, Glenn had a serious learning curve when we had our first daughter. I was not a pro, but I had experience with children before having my own. I knew what a father should look like because I had such a great example from my dad. My husband not having that meant he bumped his head several times and pretty much learned as he went. He was great at being attentive to each child's need and learning their styles.

Glenn gets major kudos because he is trustworthy, he will not abuse them, or belittle our daughters, he will be supportive, encouraging, and since birth

Melvina W.

he has and will always be there for our daughters. I remember him learning to hold them, feed them, and change diapers. I didn't have to ask Glenn to help me, he was already learning how to take care of our daughters by his own choice.

Bless his heart, he tried to be as nurturing as I would be, BUT that part he didn't pull off so good, but

has always motivated the girls instead. He encouraged them to learn from their mistakes and wise up. Talking about women's issues was never his cup of tea, and I could tell how uncomfortable he was with the topics. They didn't bother me, because I am a woman and I desired to share my insights.

Glenn could never hold a crying baby and just look them in their eyes as they fussed from being irritable. He wanted to solve problems. He would change their diaper, feed them, burp them, adjust the temperature in the room, and go through a checklist. When he exhausted every option, he would hand the babies back to me.

I loved staring into their eyes and reassuring them "Mommy got them, and everything is going to be okay." Promises I made to my children in these intimate moments I have kept to the best of my ability. Nothing they went through with me was intentionally malicious. I wanted to give them the best that I got, "No, it wasn't peaches and cream, but it was all heart."

When Life Heats UP

Glenn has always been good with his hands and solving problems. Anything that broke in the house, he was the first one to find a way to get it fixed. I am not a Mrs. Fix it, if it is broken I am down to pay a professional to get it done. Time is money and money is my time. Glenn enjoyed mechanically inclined work, whereas, for me, it was and remains a hard "not interested." I guess we are a yin and yang on common ground.

Deciding to take this job in Houston, which was paying $26 an hour for me to work an 8-day wrap, so Wednesday to Wednesday. Coming home weekly and seeing how life was getting on without me was scary at first. I knew Glenn, he was disciplined, loyal, and capable of doing right by me. I never questioned his loyalty, but I was worrying about us. The three months I worked this job I felt the wind drop out of both of our sails. We hated leaving each other and I tried for us not to argue because one good argument could cost us so much more.

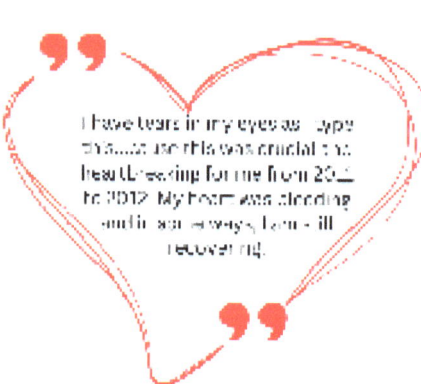

I have tears in my eyes as I type this... and this was crucial to breathe saying for me from 2012 to 2012. My heart was bleeding and it has always been ill recovering.

Yes, we had to learn how to have a relationship through a computer. Honey, we did it all. Phone sex, long calls, reflecting on our past trips, and sharing our future plans. This was not ideal and not the marriage either one of us signed up for, spending just as much time separated as together.

Melvina W.

After two months of working this chaotic schedule, I began applying for more jobs to see what doors would open for us. Keep in mind, our oldest was 14 and the twins were 11 years old. The travel was getting expensive, and the bills were being trimmed down but they were growing. I remember when I applied for a job in Boston, to get to the interview, we had to borrow money to book the flight.

I went to that interview with my life on my sleeves, and I got it. I wanted this job to bring some relief, but it brought more drama and frustration to begin with. I had to roommate with strangers and live in a house that wasn't mine, and the three houses I lived in over the course of 3 months all had mice or rats running around. I don't do rodents, but I had to do what I must because the company wasn't paying a relocation fee, unfortunately.

I did feel frustrated with Glenn and our situation at this time because I wanted to be home, and I needed things to be better financially. I know it wasn't just me who saw the problems, and it was a lot on my shoulders to steer the house back to the center during this time. Just living out of a suitcase and missing my family had tears in my eyes many nights. Sometimes, they were there because I was mad at Glenn, frustrated with myself, or because I hated the circumstances.

I was living like a single woman and I hated every moment of it. I wanted to be home. I was a mother and a wife, but I felt cheated sometimes when I had to take the lead. They may never understand my sacrifice for them (my husband and children), but I do realize my physical absence in the home did put severe strain

When Life Heats UP

on our relationship. Back at home, my daughters began to resent my calls, give me the cold shoulder, and even accuse me of being "mean" to their father.

I felt like they began to pick sides between their parents and no longer saw us as a unit. We have always been a nuclear family, but my absence did build up resentment, and I do regret that. I didn't see another way to get what we needed done, and I don't apologize for having to work, but I never wanted to lose my bond with my children.

"Back at home, my girls missed me - AND they had no idea HOW MUCH it hurt me to be away from them. How I missed my husband - trust and believe. I missed the entire situation back at home that I had built....even the damn dog, Precious!!"

I have tears in my eyes as I type this...cause this was crucial and heartbreaking for me from 2011 to 2012. My heart was bleeding and in some ways, I am still recovering.

I left home to make more money and to provide a better financial situation for my family. I had the assignment to get us out of debt and gain more experience within my industry - medical coding was the way. I left home to advance my career basically...but the price I had to pay as a mother was astounding. I don't think anyone can ever prepare themselves for the tradeoffs in life, we just have to learn how to deal with them.

Money is flowing because I never left my job in Texas, and adding the extra income from the Boston job meant I was making over 100k a year. I was able to work one of the jobs remotely, so keeping up with both wasn't too much of a challenge for me. Feeling relief and acknowledging my accomplishment of catching up on the mortgage along with other bills was a great feeling.

Glenn was a fantastic and supportive partner for me while I built my career. And no, he wasn't a stay-at-home dad chilling and not making money. He was also working and after some years bought a house. He eventually earned a hefty living also, but he slowed his progress to help support the girls while I built my career. I noticed the notes I provided in their lunch boxes, the gentle words of correction I would give to Glenn about paring his clothes together; or how I would help my daughters pick the right outfit for an event, their father couldn't do. That voice in the house was not there.

I would help my daughters through their homework and make surprise visits to the school to check in with teachers and shock the girls. I was the reinforcement, but building my career in some ways came to "bite me in the BUTT!!" When I would come home, they would feel that money was more important to me than them. They just didn't understand that without money, the lifestyle we afforded wouldn't be there. Their security meant I had to work hard to dig us out of the ditch.

I know what it is like to put your all into helping someone, and they give you their "ass to kiss." I love my daughters, but I am not going to do that for anyone. YOU can express how you feel, and if I am at fault, you might get an apology from me. But I am not falling on no sword to make people happy. I saw that my daughters were hurting, and it pained me to my heart. To this day, I still experience bouts of disconnect with the girls. I feel sometimes, they enjoy what I provide, but they do not appreciate what it costs me. Maybe they will never understand–until they have their own children, the trade we have to do for money and time to ensure their living.

It hurts when people draw the wrong conclusions, the babies I looked into their eyes and made promises to while I was away (and perhaps in some ways today) believe I didn't love them enough to stay with them. While I see it as "I loved them too much to stay. If staying meant instability, I felt that had to be more weighed into the situation." It was never easy, and anyone who thinks a mother and wife being away from her family is something she enjoys - trust me "They are smoking crack! Somebody is hitting a pipe!" - like I clearly stated it was not easy!.

My daughters are wrong if they believe money is more important to me than them, but they are not wrong to say money is important to me. I understand that money is a tool. Without it, bills don't get paid. The cars they got on their birthday would not have been purchased. The cell phones they used to probably talk bad about me to their friends when growing up couldn't have happened. As I stated earlier, the trips we took to Africa, England, Italy, Turkey, Amsterdam, France, the Caribbean Islands, and more would not have happened without the work.

I want to tell you that growth is painful, and stretching to achieve your goals doesn't always feel good. It hurts often times before it feels good. I was doing so well financially that I bought a second house, and I was proud of myself. But I realized some of my joy was shared alone. My husband and I were doing great, but my daughters let out how they felt about my parenting in 2022 and nearly stopped my heart!

How could my actions be so misunderstood I do not know. I thought I was doing good with the phone thing, only to find out years after the fact how terrible my three daughters thought I had done. I remember this conversation like yesterday, I asked them, "What children have you raised? What husband have you supported? What marriage have you kept together for almost 30-plus years?"

I then replied to the gestures with, "So if you have nothing to say, have never been married, no job making any kind of money, you don't pay any bills, but you live off everything I have worked hard to generate, how then can you judge my actions when you benefited from all of it?"

After that conversation, I did apologize for not being there, but never for sacrificing what I needed to in order to take care of them. I also apologized for the hurt they have felt over the years. I did something I don't think old-school parents have ever done, I explained my actions and where I was coming from. One thing I will never tolerate, no matter how grown my children think they are, is disrespect. The moment you get froggy enough to cross me in my house, it is time for you to go.

Something I had to do with my "twins" was "kick them out of the nest for two days. It was for their own good that I kicked them out and for my peace of mind too. Eventually, they moved out on the right terms. Glenn never wanted me to let the girls move out, he felt it would be hard on them, but life is hard. If my daughters now felt capable of bad-mouthing my decisions, it only seemed fair for them to make their own decisions. The disciplinarian in me did rise up on Mother's Day of 2022, and it took me a few days to calm down.

    My daughters were not ready for my reaction because I guess they thought their feelings justified their actions toward me. I did not agree–and yes, I was vocal and took swift action. I had everybody stand up and line up–even Glenn, Oh Yes!, to make sure they heard me clearly. I became a drill sergeant at that moment, and I knew my voice was carrying, but I did not care. No, this wasn't the first time, but it would be the last time I would be disrespected of this caliber in my house. Now that they are grown my reactions had to level up, and they did quick fast, and in a hurry, for real.

    I wanted them all to hear me clearly on that night. "I may NOT be perfect BUT I am giving you the best that I got...I HAD to go and make this money to advance my career, or we would have been on the street looking at other people's houses and collecting cans or something...I had to operate with such conviction, determination, aggressiveness, "Come Hell or High Water I had TOO…PERIOD!"

    "None of you have made the sacrifices I have had to make, but we are all dealing with them, I understand. LET this be CLEAR, because of my ACTIONS, we are all talking in this half-a-million-dollar house. The three of them got cars on their birthdays that they still drive, and Glenn I helped to support your career ambitions too. Now, you all want to make me out to be the bad guy?" As I stared at their blank faces, if they weren't blank, the feeling of their strong disapproval made me see nothing. I was not going down without a fight. I would not allow them to tell me I was a bad parent when everything they have I bought it. When every need they had, I supplied.

Yes, Glenn and I worked together on things, but these girls had nothing to do with that. I am not sitting down quietly, NOPE, while these children judge my actions with nothing to compare them to. It only seemed fitting that I told my girls right there at that moment, "Girls, you need to pack your bags and go. I am KICKING you OUT right now! I have yelled, I have cried because of all the sacrifices that I have made that you do not have a clue about!"

I told them, "Yall want to be GROWN and make women's decisions when you don't know anything about adult life, it's time for you to get up out of my house. There will only be one Alpha Female, and that is me. This is not a democracy but a dictatorship today. I am a FULL GROWN woman over here…and if you want the rain, you are going to have to deal with the mud, lighting, and the entire thunderstorm over here with me…"

To be continued…

When Life Heats UP

Motivation

Now we are getting to the meat and potatoes. You know, my top three motivators are family, love, and money. It has not been a walk in the park for me and I am sure it has not been one for you either. No one promises we will have a silver spoon in our mouths, and I am not going to feed you any soup. What I want to point out, I didn't share my personal life with you to air out bad laundry, embarrass myself, or throw anyone under the bus.

It takes guts, courage, and a strong desire to connect with others to be vulnerable and open yourself for others to draw near to you, embrace you, or judge you. I commend you for getting to this phase of the book. If you haven't noticed how much this book will help you in your personal and professional life, this is when the book turns to your narrative and story.

My daughters may not think I am as amazing as I think I am, or perhaps you believe too. No, I am not the easiest person to deal with, I have standards. Have you noticed that anyone with standards tends to have a hard time getting along with others? I don't mean you are the mean person on the playground taking everyone else's things, but you are the one enforcing the rules, and some people don't like it.

In your life, as you turn this corner, be prepared to have some of your closest family members reject your progress. It hurt like hell to be confronted by my children, but I learned something in that moment, "Never do something for someone out of vain obligation." Everything I did for my girls I did because I loved them. I didn't do it for them to give me applause, but it would have been nice. We all want to be appreciated.

I would further say that I wanted my girls to see my actions and see love in them. Do you have something or someone you want to see your actions, words, gifts, or the quality time you spend with them as valuable? The most important thing to me is time because we can never get time back. I try to maximize every second, and as a business owner, the best ones limit waste.

To avoid wasting, you have to look at what you would throw away as something another person couldn't live without. For example, when we do the first press for olive oil, we then do another press that is less refined and sell it for less. We keep making oil that is a less desirable color, favorite profile, and quality arguably, but for some people, that is okay.

When I was growing up I wanted nice things but my parents never saw the value in them. They would say things like, "There are more important things in life, Marie, than purses, clothes, and shoes." But do you know one of the pillars of any economy is clothes?

Melvina W.

Sometimes, your instincts are right, even if it takes your knowledge time to catch up. Every society since the fall of Adam and Eve has needed clothes.

No matter if you want to be covered with fig leaves, designer, boutique, or the local department store's line, you will need clothes. There are three other pillars of society shared by Dr. Robert Thomas in the book Turn Key Solution Book and Course by author K. Lee. As we live, we are expected to marry life experiences with our natural gifts. Your natural talents will make room for you!

I have always had an eye for finer things, and I never saw the life I was living as the way I would live as an adult. I wanted options, and I knew education gave me options. One of my biggest motivators growing up besides my three pillars of family, love, and money, is my personal desire for something different.

Some people may call you bougie, but your desire for finer things can serve as a healthy reminder to do better. I remember being asked in an interview, "Melvina, How did you know what you wanted out of life?" I used to think I needed a clever answer, something that sounded really deep, but I realized my answer was simple. Money.

I know the Bible thumpers are going to come after me on that one, but hear me out and put away the pitchforks. The Bible says, "Money is the answer to all things," does it not in Ecclesiastes 10:19? So if money answers all the things we need, why do we run away from it and treat financial success as the devil? I don't worship money, but I do respect it.

Motivation

If you have taken the time to build something of value and I need what you offer, I am going to regard not necessarily how much money you have but the effort and mastery exemplified. Great skills and work ethic will always bring money. Before I got to this level of having my personal driver, maid service, landscaper, etc. to do choirs I never wanted to do, I had to see a way to make that happen.

I never saw that I would be performing these functions growing up. I would call it out, "I want a maid to do this for me. I am not cutting grass in the hot sun, our ancestors already did that and it didn't look fun." I want to live life and do it from a perspective that acknowledges their great work.

Everyone that has gone on to do something great needs an example. Even Christ Jesus needed God the Father to direct his path! So what makes us think we are going to live life without a mentor, a guide, a person who has accomplished something that we give reverence to? Money is always a paper trail that leads to a wise person. Sometimes, the wisdom is in creating the product, other times, and often, it is in marketing the product and taking a raw product to make something of greater value.

I didn't always know what I was going to make of my life, but I always knew what I did not want for sure! A 9 to 5 job, barely paying my bills, and pulling me away from my family was not what I wanted. I needed money because it was a tool to help me become the mother I wanted to be. I wanted my children to travel and have nice things. I wanted to set them up in life so they wouldn't start from scratch or behind the 8 ball as I did in many ways.

I don't fault my parents for my upbringing or my struggle because they did the best they could with what they had. One of my favorite sayings is rooted in a continent I love, Africa; they say, "The children are to stand on the shoulders of their ancestors." When I first heard it, it was a mind-blowing epiphany dancing in my heart. Yes, I have one, and it works well.

It told me to work hard but not harder. Don't just be smart, but smarter. I wanted to work smart and with intention, not just aimlessly hard. I went into computers because I had a knack for mechanics and tinkering with things like my father. I didn't want to go into the automotive field, but early on I saw computers as a growing business and more light on my hands. Working on computers, I knew I could travel and be anywhere in the world and still get whatever work done I needed as long as I had the internet.

I am not a dog, and chasing my tail has never been my thing. I want to stand on the shoulders of not only my parents but also other role models who have planted seeds within me, and I dare say that the world will not forget. Before we move on to who my mentors are, who are examples to everyone, I wanted you to know this.

If you have dreamed of being a six-figure earner or higher, you are not crazy. You don't have to slut your way to the top to get there. I fit a lot of descriptions to where people would think "no's" are justified, but I said, "Yes, Melvina, we are doing this." When people told me, women don't do computers, I said, "Melvina does. So I

Motivation

guess women do computers."

    I had to be okay with being a team of one if I had to until the rest of the world caught on, and boy, haven't they done so. I am grateful to be able to share this aspect of my story. Because your mindset is truly everything. What you think you will become. If you see great things, you will become great. If you dwell on negative outcomes, they will manifest.

    If you are thinking of negative ideas and outcomes that are chasing your dreams into the ground, stop hunting and shooting down your success. Let your ideas, creativity, and innovation pull you out of the slumps. I will talk about how you get pulled out of the rabbit hole if you fall in.

    For me, most of my goals have been accomplished. However, I have not ceased to make more goals to accomplish. Education and health goals are revised repeatedly for me, as I am sure they are for you also.

    So, who are my favorite people of all time? I have to say my early motivators would start with Harriet Tubman. I know we all get those black history month assignments that we have to research. I enjoy learning but can't say that I ever enjoyed reading. I read to solve problems or get solutions and not for recreation.

    This project in school, however, was one of the first I really enjoyed. I chose to do my report on Harriet Tubman. If I had to coin my personality in history, Harriet would be the one. Harriet was bold, I am sure loud, fierce, but understood the quality of life and freedom.

Melvina W.

This woman did so much for her people, and claims are unclear as to whether or not she freed 100s or 1,000s of slaves. My question is, does any of that matter really? This woman we know freed a handful of people at a time because she had to travel in low numbers. Every time she puts her life on the line to return and set more free I call that a triumph.

A woman, during slavery, helping to set men, women, and children free is beyond bold and heroic. She had an assignment that was more important than the risk of her dying. She saw every life as needing to be saved. I know people have said Harriet didn't say, "I freed 1,000s of slaves and could have freed a 1,000 more if only they knew they were slaves." I may have gotten the quote wrong, social media is not always the best with accuracy, but agree that she meant that!

What I love about social media, it allows people to share their thoughts, and those thoughts can challenge institutionalized education and religion. Let me ask you the question: Do you believe a woman who came back and forth to free slaves on a route that could have gotten herself and every man, woman, and child killed, was a light-hearted person?

Do you think for one moment, this woman did not act like Black Moses from the Bible, her nickname? She was called 'Black Moses' because she had a resemblance with a similar cause to free her people. The same issues Moses dealt with, she did, too. People who wanted to go back. People who haven't ever been anywhere telling her which way to go.

She carried a gun for several reasons, one to

shoot someone who threatened her, including dogs. Two, to shoot anyone who double-crossed her and thought to leave and could expose the group. Harriet had a let's go forward only mentality. She wasn't turning around and she wasn't losing her life on this dangerous journey.

I know we may not think we are in danger today, but our mindset is conditioned to stay in our place in society and we have to break the chain. I don't know if Harriet freed thousands or hundreds, but I know she freed people. When I thought about writing this book and launching a course to help people, I didn't set a number, I was just walking in my assignment.

I believe the quote is true, because a natural example and many things in history point to a similar ideal. If you chain an elephant with its impeccable memory, do you know if it is constantly on that chain that restriction is ingrained into their minds, even when the chain comes off! It won't move because it still believes it is bound.

What areas in your life have you bound? What childhood experiences, traumatic events, or limitations on what you can do or achieve have you stuck in place? Mine was poverty, limited resources, and wanting more for my family, but yours may be different.

Our stories don't have to be identical. I wasn't a slave outside picking cotton, but I know what it is like not to own your own time. To feel obligated to work jobs that didn't pay enough, that had you scraping money together to get by. I didn't like it, in fact, I learned to hate it. I hate poverty, maybe that is why I love money.

Melvina W.

I see what poverty does and it should not be synonymous with the black experience. We have to see the good work done by Harriet and be confronted with the truth, there is no excuse for why we cannot change our communities from right where we stand!

You don't have to go all around the world to make a difference, you can do that in your home, on your job, in your community, and country. I promise you, if you learn to win at home, the right people will notice and come looking for you!

Harriet Tubman knocked down walls, built community, and learned to work with organizations that would help her mission. She developed strategic partnerships and helped to rehabilitate these people's lives and get them jobs. Her work didn't end when they were free, she had to coach them on what freedom is. The underground railroad wasn't just about getting to freedom but a road to living and being free.

Some of the people who left probably said, "We shouldn't have never left." There will always be people like those in the Bible who would choose to go backward to be comfortable rather than to move forward in discomfort. Right now, it may be uncomfortable for you in your home, finances, on your job, and in your business, but freedom is not about where you clock in but why.

What is your "WHY" statement? Why are you wanting to change your life? What do you want to accomplish for yourself and those around you?

I know this is not easy, freedom is not easy. It is

Motivation

an easy concept to say, but it is hard to show people the way, and it takes trust on both ends. Harriet had to trust there could be honor among thieves. These people were the proposed property of someone else. To one group, they ran away with stolen goods. Harriet freeing them, made her a thief also in the context of the law.

When our back is against the wall, the laws are wrong, you have to decide what is the ultimate law. Is it civil decency? Social norms? Political affiliations and strategies? God's thoughts, ideas, and plans?

No matter how your "WHY" statement is made, that foundation you are setting will help you affix your mind to winning. You will WIN! Come Hell or High Water, if you have to go to the hottest places, the most severe of circumstances, to help yourself or someone else, do it. The rapper Tupac once said, "Have you ever seen a Crackhead? That is eternal fire."

Some of us are addicted to substances, ideas, and ways of life that are tearing up our lives. I don't know about you, but I had to change that and with a quickness! If you are still with me, let's keep rolling. Turn the page.

Chapter 5

What it Takes

If you want to win in life, you have to take one more piece of advice from my girl Harriet, if she were alive today, I would love to meet her. You have to have a strong cut-off game. I mentioned in the previous chapter that she carried a pistol and would shoot a slave or a threat in her way without question.

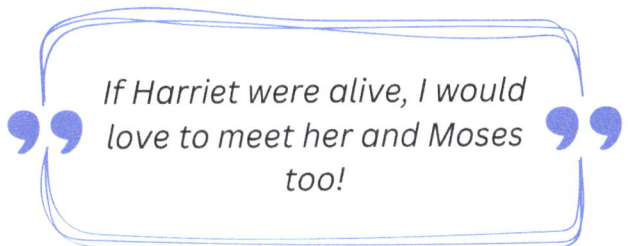

If Harriet were alive, I would love to meet her and Moses too!

If you are attached to me, we are going straight, and the next stop is financial freedom for you! We don't have time to return to old ways that leave us broke, borrowing, and to the brave or crazy stealing. We don't have to rob Peter to pay Paul, we have to align our priorities to get the most important things done first!

What it Takes

If you think you are a slave, keep it moving. If you are free or want to keep reading and picking up what I am putting down. We are living in a cutthroat time. Having a cut-off game is different from a cut-off game.

For example, that does not mean you bite the hand that feeds you. It is an oldie but goodie. We all have people in our lives who are helping us to get to the next level. KLE has been influential in writing and publishing this book. They have helped me set up my business, build my course, and launch and manage my ideas.

We are businesses, women, and sisters that are connected, and that connection is stronger than a transaction. I know she is looking out for me, and I am doing the same. Working together, I will not expect her to have a cutthroat angle towards me in the future. I know she is going to blow up, and she knows the same for me. When I aspire and accomplish my goals, she is part of that goal.

We cannot throw people away because we don't need them anymore because someone else we know may need them. Dr. Lee is very open that her company helps launch small businesses and automate sales and customer service processes. As my company grows, some of her services she says will need individuals or companies to run as I scale. I love that she is not limiting me or trying to fit me in a box but showing me how to level up! Please acknowledge that Dr. Lee and I do not have a scarcity mindset; we BOTH have an abundance mindset. PERIOD.

Melvina W.

You need people in your life who are not afraid of your success and growth. We all know of that manager, family member, and I use the word loosely, friend who doesn't want to see us do better than them. These are not people that should be part of your inner circle.

> Please acknowledge that Dr. Lee and I do not have a scarcity mindset; we BOTH have an abundance mindset. PERIOD.

Your inner circle is the people you want to become more like. You can learn from and pour into. I don't know everything, so what I don't know and need to do, I go and search for masters in that space. You don't have to go get the biggest fish to start with, you can start with a smaller one. As you grow, you will level up, and you need to move on without burning bridges.

Dynamic companies should be able to scale with their clientele also. I love how my journey in business has shown me the leveling-up process. When I started as a coder, I was coding anything people would throw my way. Yes, it was a learning curve to go into different industries and code. Similarities can exist between processes, but to do the work, you have to be willing to learn.

As you learn, don't be shocked if you have to pay to learn. We all want to get paid, that is why we seek

What it Takes

out education. But if I hadn't taken that medical coding course and done well, I am not too sure what kind of coder I would be today.

If I were too busy clutching my purse and giving excuses for why I couldn't afford it or do it, I would have nothing. I had a husband, a house to pay for, three girls and two of which are a pair of twins. My life wasn't easy for me or my husband, as I have already shown you. I went into these details because it is hard. Starting a business does require sacrifice, and if someone tells you it doesn't, they are lying.

We put money into a business with no guarantees. We don't know for certain we will be able to move anything, sell, or book appointments. We are praying that happens. If you are smart about business, you are going to ensure your business has a fighting chance by teaming up with a mentor, having partnerships, a business strategist, or a company to help with services is also essential.

I know we hate bills, but some we have to pay. I hated paying my light bill when I was broke, but I quickly realized I hated sitting in the dark more. You have to get to a point where you hate poverty. You hate performing at a level beneath what you desire. You have to set your mind on winning and getting out of life what you envision.

So, what are you seeing in your private eye? Are you seeing yourself married? Love that keeps going. I couldn't tell you what my life would be like with my husband. He does many things well, and when your day is downright terrible, there is something they can do for you that money cannot provide! Anyhow, let me stay focused or keep you focused. This book is about you, right?

Okay, so you see yourself married, or even if you are single. Write that down. Do you see yourself working where? What are you doing? Where do you live? Are you traveling? Think on these things and I want you to do me a favor, write it all down.

If you are crafty or like doing projects, I want you to make a vision board. Do you know that 82% of businesses that have a vision board complete more than half of their items? 76% of business owners say they like where they are and attribute the vision board to how they got there. The vision board is a nice way of saying strategy. What do you want for your business, and how are you going to get there?

The business strategy should be part of your personal plan also. What do you want and how are you going to get it takes a strategy. Please do not open your business and think things will just fall into place. They will not. You have to work, and for many of us, work hard as we work smart!

Another woman who has my heart, but most importantly, my eye on her moves, is Oprah, the first black billionaire I met and took a picture with. I hugged her around her neck when I met her. She probably thought I was a serious fan or I was going to put her in a headlock. Hahaha. But no, I love her business sense. She didn't allow the stereotypes to stop her from making money.

Oprah came as Oprah. She came with her dark

What it Takes

skin, strong opinions, body type, and big hair. I have been dark all of my life and have never been skinny. We all need representation in every facet of our lives, and I needed to see Oprah for a number of reasons. I needed to know that I was enough. I could sit at the table. Also, hearing no's would not discourage me or change the goals I have for myself. I was determined before, but after seeing her doing what I wanted, I became unstoppable.

We are back to the topic: who is your mentor? Who is pouring into you regularly? Is it your mom, dad, sister, pastor, friend, or foe? Yes, we listen to people who don't like us. I don't recommend it because these people are dream killers. They come into our lives to discourage us and keep us down. Don't let anyone put their thumbs down on you. You are not an ant or a small voice that can be ignored!

I am loud, always been that way, and it won't change. One because I am hard of hearing. Growing up, it was a challenge, but I learned to live with it. I speak loudly, not because at first I wanted to be heard, but because I couldn't hear all that well. Some things you do, I am sure, are learned behaviors from you having to adapt to your style or overcome your challenges.

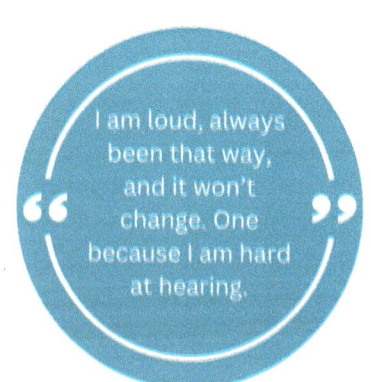

Now, when you look at your vision board, be honest. You will see that some of your expectations and needs differ from what you have. We hire people. It is good to be clear. You don't have to be mean or road, but specific is the key.

I remember having to fire my landscaper. I liked the guy's personality, but his work was not his best attribute. He could be a salesperson, but he was not good at leveling grass, pruning bushes, lining the edges, or being on time. When you see a lot of red flags, don't ignore them. Don't get along to get along. The cut-off game has to kick into effect.

Do you think Oprah got to where she is today because she kept people in her circle on sympathy? I am sure she had to fire people on her team. Unfortunately, being a boss means looking at who is progressing on your team and struggling. Then, you have to look at whether it is education, motivation, or willpower. In some aspects, you can be patient with their learning, but in others, is a strong no.

You cannot hire someone in sales who is not sales-oriented. Being sales-oriented is not limited to seeing people as dollar signs, but their why has to make them want to get people involved. If you are a pastor and want to save souls or whatever, you will be motivated to tell everyone you know, not because of money, but because you don't want them to go to hell.

Business can be that simple, too. Whatever your why, you want to help people, see them win, make money, change communities, impact children, or whatever has to push you to talk to people. Sales is not a big scary beast, it is conversations and your why being defined.

What it Takes

With Infinity Health Information Management (Infinity HIM) and Infinity HIM School, I have implemented an eight-week medical coding program for any potential persons who would like to break into the health information management field, i.e., medical coding. I have changed the paradigm by teaching medical coding and tools needed to focus on a specific type of coding to create subject matter experts for faster turnaround of employment for my students. To have a business, you don't have to make it complicated, but be specific.

Hence the reason, I have helped to get my students employed and assisted them with gaining experience and advanced knowledge of the medical coding world. I offer training, education, resume assistance, interviewing techniques, consulting, and job placement where people can work remotely while earning a great income!

www.infinityhim.com
www.infinityhimschool.com

My services are most needed within hospitals, doctors' offices, and any medical institution that sees patients. Every medical facility, no matter how large or small, has to have medical coders to code for them to receive payment for their facility and the services physicians perform. In addition to the medical coder, these entities have compliance and auditing departments as well. But why do they have those departments? Because integrity and work ethic matter. During an audit a company can discover a lot about their services, workers/contractors, and how they are issuing services.

A lot of companies don't realize they need help or additional staff until they take inventory. If you have worked in a store, then you know all about the importance of inventory. In real-time, if people come into your store expecting to have an experience or buy a product and it is not there, people can fall out.

Do you remember the crazy thing that happened years ago about a chicken sandwich? The sandwich must have been bewitched because someone got shot. We have heard the saying, "It's so good to slap your momma," but so good to get shot by somebody was news to me. If you haven't heard about the person foolishly shooting someone over a chicken sandwich, it may not be worth the time to look it up.

The point is we have to value our customers and workers/contractors and ensure they have what they need to survive. I am excellent at providing my team with support so they can do their jobs. If they say we need a product or service, I am buying it. If they need training, I will provide that, too. Lastly, questions: I am quick to provide the answers or solutions. Discovering problems is never, ironically, a problem, this process helps you find new solutions to provide services better.

If right now you have workers/contractors and

What it Takes

customers who don't value your time, it might be the right time to review how they fit into your vision. In my line of work, people try out many different fields before they find the one that sticks. I get that. I went to many different industries for coding until I decided to stay in medical coding.

I remember trying my best on a job and not being enough. The first knife to my heart happened when I thought I was doing good but got a pink slip. When I got it it was a huge hit to the ego for sure, but even bigger to my pocket. If you think getting a job is all you have to worry about, think again. There are stages to everything.

After getting fired a few times, I learned and started to filter the jobs. It was no longer up to them if I stayed but to me. When I landed the travel job and the one in Jacksonville, I chose to leave, not the other way around. Don't get discouraged if you get fired from a job. Let it motivate you to find the position or company made for you.

I wouldn't be able to talk about the firing I had to do if it never happened to me. Some people I know may think I am hard, but being hard on people can bring out the best aspects of them. I am not impossible, I will tell you that. I remember a contractor told me about a family member being sick.

You know that is one of my top priorities, and I am no hypocrite. If I would tell myself to take time off to not bring down service or the team because I have to tend to my family, I would. I told this young lady, "What do I need to do? Do you need some time off to get things sorted with your family?"

She said, "No, everything is fine, and I will get my work done." After her answer, I assumed all was well. It wasn't, but two weeks later, she came up with the excuses. I am not able to hear your excuses if I ask do you need help and you tell me "no." If you do need help or if there is an issue on the job, communicate.

I can't say that I had this experience, and the firings I got, for the most part, I understood. Firing is not a diss to the person but is a necessary stage in business to maintain standards. This young lady thought that because I was pleasant, I could empathize with her family situation and that I could bring my standard down for her. Unfortunately, I could not, and I fired her.

It is like a dagger in the heart when you fire people you wanted so desperately to work out. When I fired her, I had tears in my eyes, it hurt so badly to let her go. But she wasn't able to do the job, and I had to get the work done. People are more than a job, I will always say, but money coming in keeps us all paid.

I know this might sound strange, but empathize sometimes with the managers you have. It is not easy having to hold a bar if that means your friends and family will be bypassed in the process. The failing is like you failed, too. I started the Infinity HIM School because I wanted to give people a chance to reinvent themselves. I was fired–many times and had to fire contractors also. It feels good to find a way to give back somehow.

With Infinity HIM, I help to train students to find solutions for companies. Finding the money is a

What it Takes

skill and every company needs quality staff that can do it. This field has great pay and benefits. When you are good, you can get more done and aspire to great heights. I am always looking for students or aspiring coders who are ready to work, but even more so, those who want to pursue their "why."

     I take my staff on international all-expense paid trips. I don't think bad news, criticism, and judgment should be the only time or pieces of information you share with your team. Some of your time should be on having fun if you want to stand a chance with building a family. Getting close to people can make it hard to do what needs to be done for the business, but you are human.

Melvina W.

My best photos in 2022

Picture Section

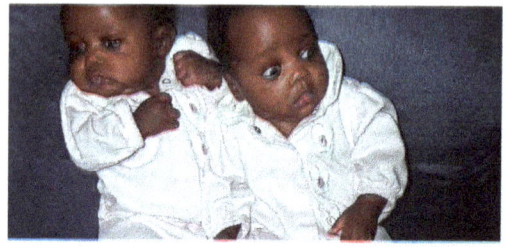

Melvina W.

Melvina W.

Melvina's Travels

Picture Section

Melvina W.

Picture Section

Solid Foundation

I know the last chapter got a little mushy, I am a woman but don't get it twisted as women, we have to maintain a standard. You may be going through a tough time, but business is still business. By upholding your standards, over time, some things will not faze you either.

I want to tell you why I can understand people but disagree with how coworkers, family, or friends want you to empathize with their situations. Don't think I am a Scrooge when you read my thoughts, I promise you, when you adopt these principles, you will completely understand their importance.

When I had a contractor, as I told you, she told me about her aunt dying. I instantly felt compassion, yes, but I also had to put my business hat on. My responsibility said to me, ask her, "If you are going to take some time off for family, how can I ensure my responsibilities are protected?" You may say, "Wow, Melvina, the woman just told you her aunt is dying; that's all you can think about?"

Solid Foundation

Now, we need to be fair to me, "The first thing I thought of was her and her aunt. The second is how her life change impacts my business. Third, her life change can also impact my family, so in short, I thought of my three pillars to my "why" statement: love, family, and money. I am constantly keeping my why statement in front of me no matter what is happening around me. We all have to do what we must, but we all also have the right to make our own choices.

So if she says to me, "All is fine," my simple reply is, "Carry on. Do what you need to." For me, that is support. Here is what happened afterward. The young lady did not have her work done. She did not communicate prior to the deadline, she was even running behind. Now, we are in a clutch, and she is asking for mercy and understanding.

This is not fair, in business, be prepared for that also. Consider this: I know I have some raised eyebrows after what I just said, but hear me out from my perspective. You come to work, you work your 40 hours for the week. Most of my people can work 30 hours and get the same pay because I am all about getting the work done!

So you bust your butt working the hours, doing your work well, and then on payday, I say to you. "You know, worker, I really appreciate you." You respond, "Oh, thank you I appreciate that, I really do." Then I hit you with, "But things have been a bit slow around here for me. My uncle just died, and I won't be able to run payroll. I will try to get to it next week, but I just need some time."

What worker do you know will say, "Oh, it's

Melvina W.

okay, I understand. Take all the time you need. Let me know a good time to come back and get paid, whoo, whoo, whoo?" I can answer that question with an honest answer. Nobody will understand not getting paid because you had a death in your family.

Owners go through things, too, children acting crazy, marital problems, clients not paying their bills, and the list goes on. One thing we cannot say to workers and expect people to understand is we cannot pay them when we have a problem. We all have the same track mind when it comes to our paycheck, "I understand life is hard for you, but what does that have to do with me? I need my money, or x, y, and z will happen."

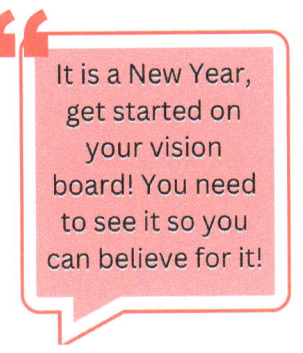

It is a New Year, get started on your vision board! You need to see it so you can believe for it!

Explain the double standard that workers want owners to pay them for not showing up to work and then expect to keep their jobs. If I have to find someone else last minute to fix their mistakes, I now have to pay two people for the same job. If you are a contractor, there is risk involved. Typically, you don't get insurance, paid days off, etc., because you essentially work for yourself. Being a contractor is freedom, but it is also a lot of responsibility.

When I first started working as a contractor, I wasn't too sure how to feel about it. Coming from the hospitality space, it was not too bad. Being a server, I was used to making my own money and making the money I wanted to make happen. I set goals, and I was

Solid Foundation

intentional about attaining them. Goals make you focus, if you haven't completed a vision board for this year, please get on that.

Being responsible for how you will make a living is always going to be challenging and threatening. When you have no guarantee, you need faith, hope, and a dream to remain hopeful when things are not looking too good. There were numerous times when I had my last, and a job would pop up. These moments told me the value of saving.

Whenever I could work, I did because I knew for every season of plenty, there could easily be a season of drought. But bills don't seem to have a drought. Your electric bill, water, gas, mortgage, groceries, etc., always find a way to burn a hole in your pocket. If it were me and I had a loss in my family, I would pull from my reserves for a month or two until my thoughts became centered.

What I was saying to the woman was, "Sorry, I cannot live in your world. I want my money, and my work needs to be down so I can get it. I want my reputation upheld. I want to be the biggest and baddest in the health information management field. So if you are not helping me again, what would I be paying you for?"

I learned real quick in business that compassion can be relative. People understand what is in their best interest–and they should. We have to see how we can work together for sure, but if you work and I don't pay you, I understand you quitting. If you don't work, I think it is understandable that you do not get paid. I am about justice and fair treatment. Sure all things won't be equal, but there should be considerations we both make, as the contractor and owner.

I don't make apologies because I know my worth, and I demand my price. I expect you to do the same. Anything I think to buy, I ask what the price is. If I like the price and feel the item or service is worth it, I buy it. I don't care if it is a purse, service for my business, or blah, blah, blah. I am self-aware and honest about what I need.

I know some of you are holding your breath and thinking, Melvina, you are mean, but I'm not, I just don't want to wait for someone to validate me. I don't expect other people to give me what I must give myself. I need to know my life is valuable, just like my contractors. I value them, and I want them to care for me. Plain and simple, justice and fairness are what we all need.

I know excuses are available to us all! What characteristic I like about Oprah, she is a money magnet. Oprah increased her network and enlarged her net worth despite challenges on every side. Harriet, yes, had a strong personality, even though she didn't have the money. In Harriet Tubman's case, money isn't everything, but it sure does help when you need things like lights, water, shelter, an office, etc..

Oprah is the biggest and baddest in her space because she amassed money, legally, in a white man's world. Oprah did it without hiding, and she witnessed and saw it. She is doing her thing even still today and no matter if you like her personally, you cannot deny her progress. Her weight struggle was documented, but she still won in business. She didn't look like a toothpick

Solid Foundation

hosting a show, "Ya'll can tell I used to be bitter toward smaller women. Not anymore!"

Oprah encouraged me to love myself. I have had so much in common with her, from my skin color and gender to my weight. What I think I love the most about Oprah is seeing someone represent me. I eat well, but I struggle with weight, always have, but that doesn't mean I beat up myself. I don't want you to be blinded by your struggles. Choose to do what you can from where you are and not let anything shake your value.

Oprah understands that building true influence is not about taking care of just you, but others also. She's giving back to the motherland, Africa, by paying to support orphanages and the less fortunate from extreme bouts of poverty. I know it may seem unappealing to say I donate money to charities overseas, but I like to see my difference. I'm a huge March of Dimes and American Cancer Society contributor.

The reason I can relate to families struggling to raise premature babies is because my twin daughters were premature. As for cancer, I have had several family members who have died from it. Another organization I am happy to give towards projects with my sorority. Sometimes, it is playing bingo with the elderly in nursing homes, and other times, giving care packages to the homeless population. Not everything is about money.

Going over and seeing the land of Africa for myself has been one of the best experiences for me. I mean, very few things are comparable to the feeling I had given to build water wells for communities, but what I do locally, I believe, still matters. It is not about the big things you do that make the most difference but how impactful they are to others. A smile can go a long way also.

Not everything you need to see can be viewed by looking through your phone or watching TV. Check and see if you need to put the technology down so you can go and explore the world! When you travel and see how other countries cook and live, you will work to find your own balance. My strong foundation was not only cultivated by living amongst my own family, but also by venturing out to see new things and places.

Some of you have never lived the life, not even faintly, of what you dream of. You might have been raised in a simple family home, are accustomed to being appreciative of the bare necessities, and traveling was only by requirement (funerals and family reunions). I want to challenge you today. I want you to consider your foundation.

What is it that you want? What is driving you to push forward and seek the best out of life? Do you want your children to have a great life and more options? That is great, fine, and dandy, but I want to remind you

Solid Foundation

of something. Your children will grow up and go to live lives of their own. Appreciate the time you have with them as children, but remember, no one can live life for you.

You are the foundation, the solid rock or sinking sand that your dreams are built upon. Don't shrink your goals because of children and family, but find a way for them to co-exist. Yes, there are sacrifices we all have to make. Great mothers make them, and so do fathers. Life is not easy, and staying home baking cookies like "Leave it to Beaver" days is not what we can all choose if, at our core, there is more.

I am not saying there is anything wrong with being a stay at home mom, a wife, or having this lifestyle. BUT! If you know you always wanted to do something more, don't use children, your husband, your job, or challenges as a distraction. Your purpose is yours, and it should be your foundation. Being a mother can be part of your purpose. Being a wife can also be part of your purpose. Yes, your drums can also be part of your purpose!

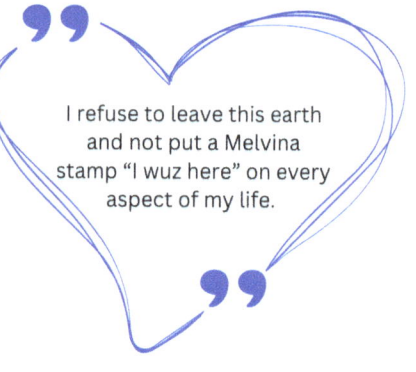

I refuse to leave this earth and not put a Melvina stamp "I wuz here" on every aspect of my life.

There are things in life I would do differently, but choosing to fulfill my purpose and live my WHY statement each day would not be a regret I have. If I hadn't chosen this life, I honestly feel my regret would have been not doing the thing I love, not earning the money needed to spoil my family with my love, and missing the chance to be the best I could be.

I refuse to leave this earth and not put a Melvina stamp "I wuz here" on every aspect of my life. Medical coding is one, sharing my story to motivate you, other women are two. Yes, I still have more to give and share and my school helps me to do that. I didn't want to help people in Africa and do nothing to help families and children here in my community.

Infinity HIM is a coding school that has allowed me to train coders in a space I am familiar with to help them change their family lives. How much would it impact your life and encourage you to know something you do, provide, or teach others can help feed their families? Can make buying not only one house possible but multiple homes.

I have been a homeowner two times. I purchased a home when I had a little money and when I had more. Money is not the issue for why some of you have not achieved your goals. I know you think if only I made more money, I could do "x, y, and z." It was when I realized my foundation was what was stopping me from obtaining what I wanted that I knew I had to shift my mindset. The first thing we must do is shift our mindset to think bigger, dream bigger, and want bigger!

Turn with me to the next chapter, Dream Big, and let me further explain.

Of course, I could not close out this chapter without including my favorite person, Oprah Winfrey! She is so inspirational to me! She was on my bucket list

Solid Foundation

to meet and I did in Atlanta – during the "Life I Want Tour." I purchased a VIP seat to ensure I hugged her neck!! OMG!! It was a great conference and a motivating time for me. To get this close to hear and accomplish what I set out to do, I became unstoppable!

Tune in to my Podcast!

"Give Me Something to Work With"

IAmMelvinaPodcast.com

I Am Melvina Podcast

Solid Foundation

Dream Big!

So, how do you get to the point where you can dream big and do the thang? You have to be real about where you are. For me, it was simple: family, love, and money quickly became my motivators. My family (husband and three daughters) is paramount in my life, and they are my loves. Without the four people I live with, this life would not have been possible for me. I cannot have one without the other – the love for and with my family is interchangeable.

So, naturally, money is what is needed to provide for that family that I love so much! To travel across the country, all 5 of us, to provide healthcare – doctors visits (I have daughters who are hearing impaired as am I, Tourette's Syndrome, Asperger's Syndrome, and more), education for colleges, cars, clothes, and more – all required money! Therefore, I am not discreet about this motivator. I love what I can accomplish with money: buying homes, paying off college, getting a chauffeur, and enjoying time with my husband. Love, family, and money provided options for me to share my abundance with my family.

Dream Big!

Time and time, I have been asked the question, "Does money buy you happiness?" I would always reply, "Yes, it absolutely does!!" I believe it "buys" your health, happiness, freedom, financial stability, a very good lifestyle, and more. Without sounding like an avaricious person, "buy" simply means it will enable you more opportunities than the norm, open more doors, and most definitely give you peace of mind for the every day 9 to 5 hustle we all do try to pay bills. I want to challenge you to believe in Infinite Possibilities.

My thoughts are, "Knowing what motivates you gives you a sense of direction. It tells you how far you came in your journey, knowing where you come from will surely tell you where you have been, and hopefully, you will now know where you want to go from here." Another strong motivator for me is always going to be education. Being educated has afforded me so much more than what my parents have had. It is in obtaining an education I was really able to Dream even Bigger!

You see, you start with your WHY statement, and then you look for ways to make that even better. I knew love, family, and money were important to me, but my WHY statement helped me to formulate a plan. I knew going back to school was the first step. When I arrived at school, I quickly noticed an associate's degree wasn't enough. A bachelor's degree wasn't enough either for what I wanted for my family, I needed a master's!

It wasn't that I set out to obtain my master's at the start of enrolling in college. As I started to get educated, I looked around the room and started doing some research, my dream had to enlarge to afford the things I dreamed of for my WHY, love, and family. I couldn't stop at having a great job and earning an associate's degree or bachelors. Even when I got a job when I graduated, I couldn't settle on one job, but I knew I needed to explore different aspects of coding.

You are likely going to experience the same thing. You will start your life on a job, and discover to get promoted, you need more education. If you want the positions that pay, you need to have the degree to demand the compensation. Don't get scared when you look at what it takes to accomplish your goals, if a woman with a hearing impairment, a husband, and three children, of which two are a pair of twins, and I worked overtime while going to school can graduate, you can too! Your journey doesn't have to be as hard as your mind, or it may not be as easy either.

Your purpose has to become worth it to you. Your picture has to become bigger! You have to dream bigger than you see or have experienced to get somewhere you have never been. Something you may not notice, we all have a dream. I know you probably have heard of the speech by the well-respected Martin Luther King Jr., "I have a Dream!"

His vision was one that went against everything our society currently represents. Yes, there were people who agreed with him, but many of them did not vocalize that agreement or stand up openly. You are going to also find that people may like your dream and want that for you, but they may not vocalize it. You may have a spouse who helps watch the children but does not shower you with positivity.

I have to say, my husband has always been a rock

Dream Big!

for me. He goes beyond what I could ask him to do constantly, and I appreciate his patience and attitude toward my success. In an interview with CereseD Jewelry blog, he was quoted to have said to the interviewer, "How do you feel about your wife's success?" (location: https://ceresed.com/blogs/news/2020-march-mag) He smiled and said, "She is smart, accomplished, and beautiful. Her words of inspiration should bring hope to millions of women! I am just a little biased as I am her husband."

My husband has been my MAIN supporter through all my years of college, job and career changes, relocating, and even picking up and moving our whole family in pursuit of my career.

People who have your back, don't throw them away. I have said it earlier, and I will say it again: risking becoming a short meme on replay. You are going to need people who can help you dream big! If it is your spouse, great! If it is your children, amazing. If it is someone at school or a person you have never met, use them to keep you focused. I told you, Oprah motivated me. I did get the chance to meet her, but even if I did

Melvina W.

not, she still played a pivotal role in my life.

What I cannot stress enough is you have to prioritize winning in your life. I know everybody has a story on why they couldn't make it or do this and that. If I leaned on my excuses, I wouldn't have anything and would feel justified in having less. I know it is not easy working two and three jobs while going to school. So go before you have to overcommit if you can. I told my daughters, don't go out here and rush to get married and have babies. Get your head on straight, get educated, and make some money before getting more bills.

I am happy to say they followed my advice, and none of them have children yet, but all are in college and doing well. I asked about your WHY statement already, but I have to ask you another question, "What is important to you?" What must you do with your life? What makes you happy? What can you not live without? These are the questions and answers you must be willing to answer.

Likewise, you have to consider your blind spots. These are tough questions and even harder answers to give. You need to ask yourself the question, "What are your weaknesses and your problematic areas in your

Dream Big!

life?" Do you see patterns in your thinking and actions that lead to results you don't want? Are there areas in your life you can and should improve on?

I am not shy about my major demons and my weaknesses in life to be and live healthier. I am continuously struggling with weight issues. Unlike other aspects of my life, I have not applied the same effort to this area as others. I am in dire need of applying my own thought process to this category of my life – which I admit I do not! Ughhh! But it is starting to change because I am doing this blog, InfiniteBeauty.blog where I share my journey of using products and services that benefit women specifically.

The same attitude I have towards business, to do my research, put a plan together, execute, work hard, and have a never give up attitude, it is my goal to apply to my health. I could use your help in this area to encourage me as I encourage you. No one is an island, the boss needs workers, the mother needs children, and the wife needs a husband.

I like to keep things simple, and dreaming big doesn't have to be complicated. I think the best plans are simple. So, if you are feeling overwhelmed right now, breathe and take it slow. Rome wasn't built in a day, and it will take time and hard work to get what you want, but you can live your dream!

As a little girl, I dreamt about being married. When I married my first husband, I had no idea what I was looking for. I was inexperienced, young, and dumb about marriage. I have to tell you, some choices we've made in our lives were dumb. I wasn't smoking crack,

Melvina W.

kind of dumb, but I wasn't the woman I am now.

The husband I have today has been married for 25 years and counting. It has NOT been easy because every marriage comes with trials and tribulations. For example, low income, relocation, the stresses of working away from home, Skype, and phone sex let us down. But we made it, and we are still making it! One thing that I have learned is that communication is VERY important, we are still dating and communicating – we both agree that divorce was not an option.

This same "Never Give UP" attitude I have toward marriage and divorce can be adopted for achieving your dreams and then dreaming bigger. If your goal is easy to obtain, your dream has not been made bigger. Your dream has to pull on you so it sharpens the areas you are weak. If I wanted to explore my next level of dreaming big, I have to be willing to become uncomfortable again. I must be willing to learn and approach the experiences with an open mind as I did for new subjects in school.

Everything you have ever done with your life is functioning as a building block to starting you on the path to achieving your wildest dreams!

Dream Big!

Starting on the Path

Sometimes, to warm up to doing something challenging, I do something else to make myself feel good about it. For example, if someone has a nail in their foot, somebody might pinch their finger to shift the focus. I'm a southern girl, so soul food is my favorite and comfort zone. I enjoy cooking and eating some collard greens, hoppin' john (black-eyed peas and rice), macaroni & cheese, fried chicken, and more. However, on a healthier tip, I love salmon, salad, sandwiches, baked and grilled items.

Pretty straightforward, right? But have you ever tried something a bit off the menu? Like rabbits, snakes, raccoons, or squirrels? I know when we think of animals that we feel should be running free, caged, or we see more as roadkill, we don't think of them as food, right? I have to admit that even though I am afraid of raccoons, I will eat one fast and in a hurry. Don't judge me as I smile and laugh at myself.

You see, there was a time I turned my nose up at the thought of eating a raccoon. That is not an animal

Starting on the Path

you will find in your deli or typical grocery store, but that little vermin tastes so good when it is cooked right. He can be tricky to catch, but a good Southern hunter can catch a few for you to try.

But why do I suggest you try something that you don't typically see as food? What is the value or moral of a story about eating something strange? What it does is expose you to see your world differently. We didn't always see chicken as food. We were conditioned to see them that way. When you think of dolphins, you don't typically see them as food, right? You see them as helpful water creatures that enjoy playing more than anything.

This perception is also a form of conditioning. Now, I want to ask the question, what beliefs have you adopted about your personal story? What do you believe about yourself, experiences, fears, likes, and dislikes is meant to help you start on a new path to accomplishing your dreams? I dare to tell you that everything you have ever done can be used to prepare the way for starting out on a different path.

For some of us, we do not have the way to do things right. If you grew up in a family that didn't have the support of both parents, married, and in love, you may be missing that element in life. It is hard to duplicate something you have not seen. It is incredibly easy to do anything when you have a guide and someone to help walk you through the changes. But what do you do when you are navigating new waters alone?

It was not easy for me to move to Boston by myself while my children and husband remained in Atlanta. I

Melvina W.

missed them terribly, and I had to learn new concepts, ideas, and measures about coding. School is good for exposing you to what you may encounter in the real world, but nothing prepares you like on-the-job training. It wasn't until I arrived at this job that I realized learning never ends. I had certificates and degrees, but working a job still felt like there was more.

My education surely set me on the path to living my dream, but the vision got bigger. I learned more about coding, the industry, and myself. I started to realize what I enjoyed about coding and what I struggled with. Having good grades in school can make you feel confident when obtaining a job. However, when you perform below standard, it quickly turns from confidence to uncertainty. I can only imagine how people feel that they graduated by a few points from failing. It can be intimidating to go into interviews or work a job knowing others have more experience and knowledge than you.

Again, breathe for me real quick. People will always be out here doing things you cannot control, but what you can impact is you. You control your destiny more than you know. You control how much you want to get paid, where you want to work, and for how long. If you don't, you need to study and develop a plan to get there if that is what you want. Whatever you want bad enough, you will find a way to get it done.

I like watching these crazy movies sometimes where it looks like the whole earth went to hell. You know, when the people lost their homes, barely have food, and something tragic looks like it has happened. It is amazing to see how people value water and food and also how resourceful people can become. The trick to life is not to wait for your world to put you in dire straits, to operate as if things are bad and must get better.

When you feel like life isn't that bad, you can become too comfortable with your circumstances. Comfortability is often your ticket to accepting less than you should. When I got comfortable with that job, I had to look at the scarcity of time I was spending with my family, and that made me become resourceful again. Don't look at what you have achieved and think, "I am good here. I am just going to chill." Before you know it, your whole life can change. They can lay you off, lose a contract, or you can make a terrible mistake and get fired!

Having a backup plan is a must if you work for anybody or yourself. There are no guarantees in life, and that means for you as well. You cannot control what may befall their future or yours. So, always assume and look for ways to make your life better. One thing I like about millennials, you don't have to tell them to look for greater things. Many of them don't stay on jobs past a few years, and that has some benefits.

By constantly moving and having a drive to

obtain more, you are equipping your mind to learn. The more you can learn and apply what you learn to your dream, the bigger your outcome can become. When I made my first 100k, it wasn't because I got complacent

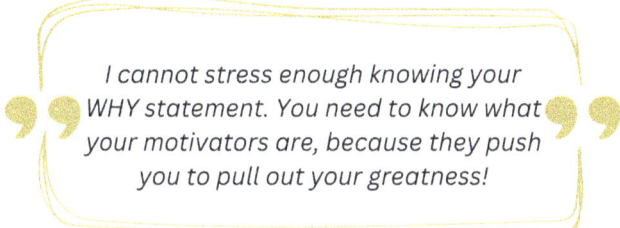

I cannot stress enough knowing your WHY statement. You need to know what your motivators are, because they push you to pull out your greatness!

with one job. It took 3 jobs working simultaneously to earn 6 figures. I valued what that kind of money could do for me. I needed to pay off my house, pay down debt, and spend more time with my family. Money afforded that for me.

What do you need, where is your path starting today? Are you needing to revisit your WHY statement? Have you become complacent? Are there factors in life you know you have been ignoring or belittling?

I am going to be real with you: if anyone or anything should be worth your time, it should be able to help you on your path. If people are not helping you on the path, cut them off. If contractors are not cutting it, you must be willing to fire them. If your mindset is not sending you in the right direction, you have to be willing to divorce your way of thinking to stay on the path.

We all want to be honest with ourselves; that has value, but sometimes you gotta speak ahead of where you are. Some people say you have to speak about what you want to happen, even before it happens, to see it

Starting on the Path

happen. You gotta believe you can have what you say so your work will not be wasted. Nothing is more pathetic to me than someone working hard and expecting nothing in return.

Honey, if you paid for it, worked for it, you better get what you deserve. Stop letting people tell you what they are going to give you and begin to demand what you will not accept. I refused to accept poverty or anything that was beneath my big dream. Let me tell you, I got it all. The husband, children, job, business, success, and money. Even if you are not the best, tell yourself you are the best! Then, pursue becoming the best.

Another thing you cannot be is too slow. I know, you probably heard this before it is you "You move too slow." Don't be slow in getting, the early bird catches the worm. You don't have to be Usain Bolt, but you better not be a tortoise when you are running up against hares. Life is competitive, and you need to have your game face on. I know as women many of us are not into sports.

I got into sports and developed a competitive nature from my father. One of the best things a father can give a daughter, I feel, is a competitive nature. The world is going to see who will survive. If there is one bottle of water, which person will get it. There are many ways to reach the bottle for sure, but the fittest will rise to the top. It might not sound fair that the big fish eats more and the small fish dies, but that is the world we live in.

To become a strong big fish, you have to learn to survive. You cannot get tired of swimming, learning, and advancing if you want to accomplish your dreams.

Melvina W.

I was a small fish when I started, then I became a big fish in a small pond, and now I am a growing fish in the ocean. I feel the limits are not there anymore. I know some of us have blinders on like horses. We only see straight and in front of us is a job, promotion, or marriage.

If only you were to take the blinders off, you would see a whole lot more going on. You don't want to get distracted, nervous, or fearful. The world will always be busy, and things will always be happening. Don't stress, learn to strategize. My husband and I had to learn to strategize when the going got tough. We couldn't quit, we had to move forward. When the bills piled on, we had to find ways to knock them down.

> Misappropriating money and time can be one of your biggest regrets.

When children needed stuff, we had to come up with how are we going to provide. If the cable went out, we had a tape they watched and were happy. Sometimes, seeing the content made us question the bill altogether. At times we can be working harder than we need to. We put higher standards on ourselves than the job even required. Look at the need to best assess what time or money something needs.

Misappropriating money and time can be one of the biggest regrets. When you do a self-inventory, look

Starting on the Path
at where you are spending your money. Look at where you are spending your time. Determine if you can better spend your money or time. In the coding world, our job is to find the money and help hospitals save. Too often we think everything we are spending towards is a necessity, only we find it is not. Some of our ways are outdated and antiquated. There are simply more efficient ways to do things.

    You don't have to hand wash your clothes anymore, there are washer machines that can do the work for you. You don't need a line to dry outside when you have a dryer. By having these machines, you gain more time. Yes, dryers shed fabric from your clothes. The sun may be the best alternative if you want to preserve clothes, but how long do you intend to keep your clothes? Most of us don't keep anything forever, let alone a few years before we give it away and buy something else.

    Times are changing, and you have to be aware of the changes and see how they are impacting you.

Overcoming Challenges

Being a quick learner has always been a skill in my bag. I would watch my father and mother do tasks, and I would pick it up whether I wanted to learn or not. On the job, I quickly learned as I made mistakes, and I was quicker to fire back the change and improvement. Being able to bounce back is a skill, but it is a learnable skill. If you are stuck in a rut, things are not going well or making sense, it is time to watch someone else who has it right.

I want to be clear you are not watching to compare yourself, that is a dumb and highly discouraging plan, you want to learn vicariously through other people's wins and failures. You can win regardless of the road you take. I have been fired and I also quit jobs when they didn't serve my purpose and goals. It is okay to shift your life, and at times, we will have to. Don't be so loyal to other people's jobs that you forsake your own purpose.

So what do you do if life is happening and you know your purpose is on a ticking time bomb ready

Overcoming Challenges

to explode? You start making realistic plans that you will implement to overcome every challenge. What you don't do is throw out excuses for why you "can't," ughh. Nothing is more annoying than hearing people say, "Oh, I can't do it, Melvina. It is impossible, blah, blah, blah." I don't want to hear it.

What I want to hear is, "Melvina, right now, with what we have, it is going to be a struggle. This and this needs to happen. We might have to buy this so I can learn this or have that." I need you to learn to be solution-driven. People who learn to overcome challenges can run businesses, grow on the job, and expand into other positions. Don't think you have to know all the answers or have everything within yourself to elevate. The truth, honey, none of us have it all. If you want to scale and make more money, you are going to spend money to get there. You may need to make a plan to go back to school, take a course, or read a book.

> Good move; I see you reading this book. I see you, Girl! Soon enough, you will get what you are working so hard for!

Good move, you are reading this one. You may be thinking, "What else can I do, Melvina?" You have to set actionable goals. You need to write it down. Don't keep everything in your mind, start putting it on paper. When you write down your goals, it makes it real. You have a standard, urgency is created, and motivation can be struck within your heart.

It is hard work starting a business, going back to school, or working to get promoted on the job. You

Melvina W.

have to be honest about where you are and see if there is anything you are doing to keep you from reaching your goals. Are you late to work? Do you do enough to keep from being fired? Are you working hard and taking care of everyone else's job and not getting promoted? If you are getting overlooked where you are, "Stop right now and start looking for where you can be."

Jobs right now are plentiful. A lot of people don't want to work, and people who are under-qualified are getting positions because the competition is not there in all fields. COVID-19 shook the world up, take advantage of it. You don't have to stay in your cubby, or you can move to your home if you search and do the work to get the job. I had to take courses to obtain the jobs I wanted. I didn't come out of college already set to get my dream job, I had to work and get trained for it.

Don't reject your humble beginnings. Don't think for a second that what you do and have accomplished is nothing. There is someone looking for everybody, but are you in the right position to be seen? Are you writing a resume that captures your skills and abilities? Are you playing down your history and understanding?

With Infinity HIM, I offer resume review, coaching, and consulting to help people who need to get a job paying enough to give them their lives back! If you know your resume is whack and you are not getting the positions you can do, come to me and let me help you. But if you choose not to, go to a professional who can help you read over your skill sets and pump them up. On a resume, it is not the best time to hold back on what you offer.

Overcoming Challenges

Another thing I must tell you is do not be afraid to put yourself out there! You will never know what you can accomplish if you don't put your best foot forward. When I first wrote my resume, I got zero calls. Then, I started to get internships and temp jobs, but the real ones escaped my grasp. I started looking again at my resume and included things I thought were no big deal. What I couldn't do in months, I started seeing the results when I embellished my skill set.

I worked a temp job and got as much experience as I could. I worked that job so hard in two months I was able to claim two years of knowledge easily. I ended up landing a job at Mayo Clinic because I was willing to work a job that would benefit my skill set to get my feet wet. Don't think you won't have to put some time in to get a handle on your career, so woman up! See the big picture at the end of the tunnel, and keep going!

Something I never forgot as I got position after position in my career, never forget where I came from. Knowing where you came from can keep you encouraged and focused as you move forward. If you never want to be broke again, don't use that as a fear but a strength. You know how to be resourceful because you made it with very little–or nothing! That has value, take that same willingness to win as you go back to school and try new things.

Find a coach and mentor who can also talk you back on the path when you jump off. For me, that person was my husband. He always said the right words to encourage me when I thought about slowing down. He would encourage me and tell me I was made to do this and was sure to win. I needed to hear what he said, even

Melvina W.

though I always believed it. It is good to hear that you are great, not because you are cocky or a narcissist, but because you want your props.

Working hard and no one taking note of it, can be discouraging. It was a huge blow to hear tough conversations from my girls over the years, but again, my husband stood with me. We together were able to build relationships and work to keep the love flowing when life issues challenged it. There will be issues that pop up, and you will need someone to help you navigate the unknown.

I help students in my coding classes and professionals who call for help all the time with coaching. I know coaching is an industry that some of us feel we cannot afford, but I want to tell you many of us cannot afford not having a coach. When you have someone in your corner who can help you shortcut a process, pay them! Yes, we can all run social media campaigns, doesn't mean we should. We can all spend time slaving to cook a gourmet meal, or we can spend the money and enjoy the food and not the labor. Choose activities that best use your time and skill.

You don't have to complete every phase to get the accolades for completing a task. Do what you can and stay focused on what matters most. If you can have a team to help push an idea through, use the team. We said two heads are better than one, but a team can give you a whole lot of hands to get the work done! Your family is the perfect training ground for launching your business or excelling in your career.

Motivating children can be one of the trickiest

Overcoming Challenges

jobs, can't it? Trying to convince people who know of your strengths and weaknesses can be a challenge to convert to clients or believers. If they are not on the same team as your plan, don't let it stop you. Get around people who see the vision. Join a group, join a club, hell, you can even take my course if it will help.

I want you to know how serious I am about being positive about your future. Negative thoughts produce lackluster results and progress. You are not busting your butt to look cute, you want results. You want sales, you want success. Get around people who can help nurture you to get there.

I also cannot close out this book without emphasizing your need to believe in Infinite Possibilities. Come Hell or High Water, you have to be determined to win! Don't think becoming a success, a millionaire, or even having a successful marriage comes without challenges. Success comes by overcoming your challenges!

You will lose friends on this road, but don't let people not talking to you discourage you. They will either come around later or not, either way, you have to be good. You must live for yourself because you cannot live for anyone else. Your children will grow up, move out, and get on. Your spouse, no matter how much they love you, cannot accomplish your purpose for you. You have to grab the horns and get it done yourself!

Do you know that even God won't do something He told you to do? If this is your assignment, your purpose, your career, your business, own it! Don't blame anyone else, point the finger to you. You are either making it happen or becoming the reason it won't happen.

Melvina W.

So make your choice, and make it count. Filter what you hear and who you listen to.

People who don't have anything are not the best people to have in your ear to show you what to do. They may be okay to show you what not to do but don't spend too much time here. Some people simply are not going where you are. They cannot help you at the level you are advancing to in ways that you may like. Appreciate them how you can, but stay focused.

Don't think you are missing out on anything because you are not sitting on the couch talking about stuff in the past. In fact, stop spending so much time reminiscing when most of the stuff in your past didn't help you advance. Don't think you are missing out because you missed parties, events, or stuff that meant you no good anyway. Sometimes you have to stay away from the club so you can make something of yourself. Sacrifice now so you can chill on the beach and have real peace.

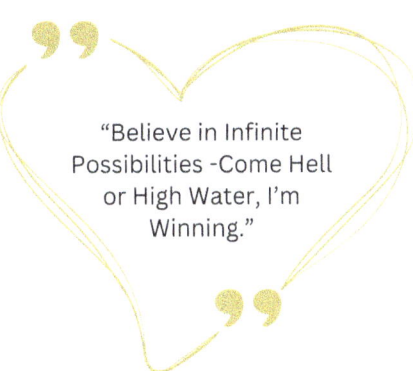

"Believe in Infinite Possibilities -Come Hell or High Water, I'm Winning."

Consider who has the biggest influence on your decisions. God put people on earth to help you, listen to

Overcoming Challenges

them. Who should you listen to? The people who have something you are trying to get.

If you ask me, I think certain degrees are a waste of time if you want to be a millionaire. I remember telling someone a degree in Business is sucky. Sure, she was offended, but that wasn't my intention. I got 4 degrees and have made over 6 figures, with ambitions to become a millionaire someday.

I am not there yet, but I am tracking in the right direction. I think she should have asked herself, What can Melvina bring to the conversation? The Blind leading the blind is dumber than smoking crack and thinking you will be a phenomenal scientist.

When you are sharing knowledge with people who ignore it or don't appreciate it, move on and stop the conversation. As I say, "Save your breath, and let them carry on." They will come back and admit they were wrong or avoid you like the plague because they are likely embarrassed. I am not a mean person, but I am very honest. I don't want to see anyone lose in life, and if I can help people avoid unnecessary debt, I will share.

I didn't write this book, create a course, or start a school because I wanted to crap on people. I did it to help women who are like me at different phases of my life. I want to help you win, plain and simple. If you leave this book with anything, leave knowing you have what it takes to live your dream and live on purpose. I must tell you again: believe in your infinite possibilities.

Resources

Congratulations on finishing this book, being intentional about your future and getting to know Melvina's story. I trust you have been introduced to several principles that will impact your life. It has taken me years to work to perfect my system for success. And as I have said, you will always be learning and must keep a teachable attitude. As such, I am always looking for resources to help me grow.

I wanted to share with you a few things I think can benefit you as you work toward living your Dream!

I have launched an amazing course to be paired with this book. Yes, you can get a double dose of Melvina with the course that helps you to further explore the principles steps in my process, and review my story. I understand hearing something once can leave a lasting impact, but having access to that material for a longer period allows you the time to implement the strategies in a practical way. I encourage you to learn more about the course by scanning the QR code.

Resources

I spoke a lot about living your dream within this book and taking risks!

Connect with the School

Of course, I know a risk shouldn't be something you do drunk on a Saturday night; it should be a thought-out plan with a solid foundation that you attempt with the best odds in your favor. I've helped many students pass training modules, progress through their medical coding programs and secure jobs for Infinity HIM School students. If you are passionate about starting a new path and grossing a stable income that can scale, learn more about how my school and coaching can help you.

Learn more about Services

Now, what about my lady friends who want to start their businesses and make the sky the limit for their earning potential? When I began my school, I knew that further diversifying my income had always been a goal of mine. I liked real estate, financial investing, and selling products or services. As mentioned in the book, I created Infinite Beauty Blog to help showcase products and services that benefit women. What I love the most about the site is we help women entrepreneurs launch their businesses on our platform and give away tips for joining Multi-Level Marketing Businesses for those interested in selling other people's products.

If you want to start your own business and begin on a solid foundation, we have partnered with KLE to help you start or grow your business. Nowadays, it makes no sense why everyone does not have a business to sell something they already use or need. Sharing your story has value. We share stories, products, and services on our blog like yours to help women everywhere.

If you need a location to showcase your products or services and include you in the blog's marketing campaign, visit the site to search our partners, shop products, and learn more about including your business.

Scan QR

Lastly, I could not let you go without discussing a Black Cup of Joe! And I ain't talking just coffee!

Resources

I am not sure if you have noticed, but the coffee business is a 17 billion dollar industry annually. Every year, billions of dollars are spent on it, you guessed it, coffee! I got to thinking: What could your household do with a fraction of that money? How could income from coffee better impact communities here in the US and abroad? Isn't it ironic that coffee yields so much money, but very little of that income comes back to the countries that produce it or the people who drink it?

Have some of these brands hosted events you have been to? I don't see any community initiatives by coffee brands, so I wanted to do something about it. I have formed a movement that you can learn more about at BlackCupOfJoe.com, where women can come together and buy and sell coffee to use the proceeds to build families and communities.

You can become an affiliate marketer of one of the brands we have partnered with, help us sell it, or buy it yourself. Every cup you enjoy goes to a great cause and supports Black-Owned businesses. Visit the QR to learn more.

Lastly, I want to mention the course that works well with this book. If you know you need to push and keep the momentum from this book, register for the course. Scan the QR code to register and learn more.

Now, what about my free giveaways? I want to thank you, of course, for reading this book to the end. If you scan this QR code, you will get a free gift I know you will enjoy and can share with your friends and family.

I look forward to staying connected with you and hearing about your success. Please be sure to connect with me by scanning the QR code. Until next time, stay away from making decisions that would make me ask, "Are you smoking crack or something?"

Melvina W.

Resources

About the Author

Melvina W is a firm believer in Infinite Possibilities! She was born and raised in Savannah, Georgia, and more than exemplifies the true meaning of going above and beyond, believing the sky is the limit.

Melvina has more than 15 years of expertise in the Health Information Management (HIM) arena. She has worked for several hospitals across the United States, from Level One to Four, Teaching facilities, Trauma and Critical care units, and many more. She specializes in several medical coding disciplines.

Melvina also acquired a passion for coding and auditing charts for several Professional Service disciplines such as Inpatient, Observations, Consults, Clinics, and more. Melvina is infatuated with validating all coding assignments, modifiers, and diagnoses to ensure compliance with the HIM arena, and she loves solving "HIM problematic edits for Federal, State, and payer-specific regulations. Melvina has proven to be a person who collaborates with physicians to improve documentation to obtain the utmost reimbursement

About Melvina Washington

for the healthcare facility. In addition to coding, auditing, and compliance assignments, she is an excellent communicator, motivator, and team player who fully completes her projects and assignments with the highest confidentiality and accuracy possible.

In addition to her work, Melvina is the owner/founder and President of Infinity Health Information Management (HIM) and Infinity HIM School, where she has implemented an eight-week medical coding program for any potential persons who would like to break into the coding field. Melvina is changing the paradigm by teaching medical coding by focusing on a specific type of coding to create subject matter experts for faster turnaround of employment for the students.

Melvina has employed and assisted her students in gaining experience and advanced knowledge of the coding world. She offers training, education, resume assistance and interviewing techniques, consulting, and even job placement to qualified persons to gain real-world experience!

Melvina has a Master's in Business Administration with a concentration in Healthcare Management, a Bachelor's in Computer Information Systems, and an Associate's degree in Health Information Technology from the University of Phoenix. She is a Registered Health Information Technician (RHIT) with the American Health Information Management Association (AHIMA). She is also a Certified Professional Coder (CPC) with the American Academy of Professional Coders (AAPC). Melvina is a Georgia American Health Information Management Association (GAHIMA) and AAPC member. Attending meetings and networking

Melvina W.

with these organizations has enabled Melvina to correspond with other leaders in the industry and better coach her students.

Melvina has been a proud member of Zeta Phi Beta Sorority, Incorporated, since 2014 and has remained a member of Sigma Mu Zeta Chapter since her induction. She has been highly active within her chapter and volunteers in various community programs. Melvina believes in the power of giving back and placed 5th for all regions for March of Dimes under the Zeta Phi Beta Inc. individual fundraiser in 2019 and first place in 2020. She is a major contributor for the American Cancer Society, serves people experiencing homelessness, and plays bingo with seniors at nursing homes, among other activities.

In addition, Melvina owns the Infinite Beauty Blog and Black Cup of Joe platforms. Both blogs encourage women to chase their dreams and buy products and services to help make their lives and communities better. Melvina says, "I am blessed and fortunate," she feels she needs to share her story with other women looking for guidance to start or grow a business. She wrote and published her first book, Come Hell or High Water, and created a course for a deeper study.

About Melvina Washington

Melvina has been happily married to Glenn Feaster for 25 years and resides in Georgia. They are proud parents of three daughters who have graduated Historically Black Colleges/Universities. The oldest daughter, Mariama Aisha is working as a Meteorologist. She has her Masters and Bachelors degree and she is also a member of Zeta Phi Beta, Inc. The twins, Sierra Leone is working as a Special Education Teacher has her Bachelor's degree and attending school for her Masters degree and Amira Nkeiruka is working as a Civil En-

gineer has her bachelor's degree. Her three daughters are pursuing their dreams using the strong foundation Melvina and Glenn have implemented. Melvina's family is well-traveled. They have visited Canada, Mexico, France, Turkey, Italy, the United Kingdom, Egypt, Ghana, Togo, Australia, New Zealand, the Caribbean Islands, and over 30 States in the US so far.

Melvina's words to live by:

> "Do not be afraid of changing the paradigm. Make your own rules and follow them. Aggressively obtain financial education and wealth to leave a more secure, stabilized infrastructure for your family lineage. Believe that education creates options so you don't become complacent with your career or life. Expect the best; however, always have a backup plan and expect the unexpected. Remember always to give back, help others grow, and develop into what you have already come; pass it forward."

"Be yourself, dream big, work hard, play harder, and believe in infinite possibilities."

Melvina W., MBA, RHIT, CPC
Owner/President of Infinity HIM School, Infinite Beauty Possibilities, Black Cup of Joe Organizer, and Published Author/Mentor
Georgia 30309
Website: Infinityhim.com
Website: infinityhimschool.com
Website: IAmMelvina.com
Website: IAMMelvinaW.com

About Melvina Washington

Website: IAmMelvinaPodcast.com
Website: BlackCupofJoe.com
Website: InfiniteBeauty.blog
Email: infinity@infinityhim.com or info@Iammelvina.com

SCAN ME

Call or Text:
770-240-0089 Press Extension 1
Web: KLEpub.com
Email Services@klepub.com

It's time to start and finish **YOUR Story**!

KLE Publishing specializes in helping people become authors. In as little as 15 to 90 days, we can help you develop your books and e-books and publish to 39,000 outlets! We also offer audiobook services.

Ghostwrite, Edit, Format, Publish
We can help from **Start to Finish.**

Explore and learn more about published authors affiliated with KLE.

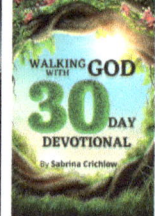

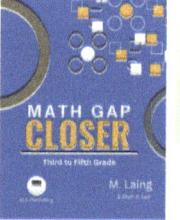

KLEPub.com

SCAN ME
Or Use Link

Connect with KLE

Services to Launch or Grow Your Business for Authors & Product or Service based Companies

Key Solution TURN

Four Departments:
- Coaching and Consulting - Business SWOT Analysis
- Writing and Publishing Dept: Writing Services, Book/Ebook/Audio Book Services
- Business Concierge: Social Media, Web, CRM, and New Business Formulation Support: Message, Brand, Sales, Product Development, Strategy
- Production: Content Creation

www.ingramcontent.com/pod-product-compliance
Lightning Source LLC
Chambersburg PA
CBHW061800070526
44586CB00023B/2648